They All Laughed When I Sat Down at the Computer

and Other True Tales of One Man's Struggle with Personal Computing

D0463984

Erik Sandberg-Diment

COMPUTER BOOK DIVISION/SIMON & SCHUSTER, INC.
NEW YORK

Copyright © 1985 by Erik Sandberg-Diment and the Getare Trust, James A. Schwarz, trustee
All rights reserved
including the right of reproduction
in whole or in part in any form
Published by the Computer Book Division/Simon & Schuster, Inc.
Simon & Schuster Building
Rockefeller Center
1230 Avenue of the Americas
New York, New York 10020
SIMON AND SCHUSTER and colophon are registered trademarks of Simon & Schuster, Inc.
Designed by Karolina Harris
Manufactured in the United States of America

10 9 8 7 6 5 4 3 2 1

Library of Congress Cataloging in Publication Data

Sandberg-Diment, Erik.
    They all laughed when I sat down at the computer.

    1. Microcomputers. I. Title.
QA76.5.S215 1985   001.64   85-5275
ISBN:0-671-52750-9

Contents

1: The Computer-Assisted Bath

Personal computing entered my life the day I was caught between Larry, our 300-pound Suffolk stud ram, and a stone wall. Ensconced in a long, hot bath that evening, soaking the bruises incurred by my discovery that the stone wall was softer than Larry's head, I began reflecting on a current article assignment I had from *Esquire*.

The year was 1976, and Clay Felker, then editor of *Esquire*, was enthusiastic about a feature on home computers I had proposed. He wanted the manuscript right away. My only problem was that, having brought the subject up, I couldn't figure out what on earth anyone would ever use a home computer for.

Beneath the futuristic media hype just beginning its ground swell over the new home computers, I had glimpsed a fascinating technology. The thought of being able to buy a machine for a mere thousand bucks or so that a decade earlier would have represented a couple of million dollars' worth of computing power was astonishing. The concept of a tiny, paper-thin wafer occupying less space than a postage stamp and doing all the incredible things computer freaks were claiming it could do was staggering.

My enlightenment concerning microcomputers began in the basement of Les Solomon's New York home. Les, editor of *Popular Electronics,* had published an article the year before describing the Altair kit, the original personal computer. On the evening in question, he had invited me over to meet Lee Felsenstein, one of the early microcomputer designers, who was flying in from California with a new home computer prototype. The Sol, Lee's walnut-cased, typewriter-sized computer, was soon to be unveiled in manufactured form by Processor Technology, and I was one of the few people to be granted a sneak preview of this innovative and technologically sophisticated machine.

New to the magic of computerland, naive about its electronic inhabitants, I asked these two standard-bearers at the crossroads of a brave new world, "What can I do with it?" The answer I received was a nightlong marathon demonstration—of shoot-'em-down Star Trek. That was all.

Today, nine years later, there are other answers to that question, though I suspect I have unearthed far from all the future holds. Yet with more than a dozen computers around the farm and, courtesy of my position as the "Personal Computers" columnist for *The New York Times,* a software reviewer's access to an almost limitless number of programs, I find that the machines have changed our family's lives very little.

My wife and children use a computer sometimes, for one thing or another, but they don't use one for all the things the early believers in computer power envisioned as accomplishments of the microminiature wonder machines. Susan, my wife, uses the computer for word processing, as do I on occasion. Rarely does she touch the machine otherwise. My two daughters, Genevieve, fourteen years old, and Tanya, eleven, are more likely to listen to the radio, read a book, or ride a horse than to run educational programs, which they find on the whole "bo-o-o-ring," or play a video game. Revell, nearly

6

five, uses leftover sheets of computer paper to make boats and airplanes and collects the perforated feed strips for streamers. I am personally against exposing very young children to computers—an iconoclastic position, I'll grant, but one that I feel has no less validity than the toddler "computer literacy" push being fostered by the computer industry. This is not to say that computers aren't fun. They are.

Life with a computer is very much like life with a car, at least in our family. Something has been added, but it hasn't become central to the household, as so many of the early prognosticators envisioned. Most of the idealized uses first proposed for the home computer, in fact, never materialized.

"You can tell the pioneers from the rest of the crowd," a Silicon Valley saying goes, "by the arrows in their backs." Like most of the early settlers of microcomputerdom, the early dreams of a computerized home wherein the machine awoke you with breakfast coffee, prepared the shopping list, monitored the house environment, and became the children's best friend, ended up on Boot Hill. I myself ended up taking a bath—literally and, as it was to turn out, figuratively. As I say, my own involvement with the new technology all began with that long, hot soak.

Lying there in the tub, I recalled the story, probably apocryphal, of how, back in the forties, Thomas Watson, Sr., head of IBM, decided that the firm should not enter the computer business. The machines were so expensive and so limited in their use, he is said to have reasoned, that the total world demand for them would probably never exceed a dozen or two.

Looking back, it's easy to laugh at his argument. But at the time he was right. No one had yet conceived of computerized payrolls, telephone billing, credit card accounts, and junk mail. No one had yet suffered nightmares featuring an Internal Revenue Service and other governmental departments bloated beyond recognition by a glut of computerized data. Nor had anyone yet dreamt of the paper chase that xerography would instigate, which is another story altogether.

When *Popular Electronics* ran its January 1975 cover story on the Altair, there was only one working prototype around, and that had been lost in the mail. The machine on the cover

7

was actually a dummy cobbled up to meet the magazine's deadline. MITS, the manufacturer of the computer, expected the article to elicit a couple of hundred orders over the course of the year. Instead, the first week following publication of the article, MITS was flooded with requests, hundreds of them, complete with checks and pleas for instantaneous delivery. The company went from almost half a million dollars in the red to a quarter of a million dollars in the black in less than a month.

Needless to say, at that point the question of availability became tenuous indeed. Most of the tiny company's efforts went perforce to opening orders and answering inquiries. Thus was born a mode of operation that was to become as much a part of the microcomputer industry as the machines themselves: announce a product, collect the money, and then start building goods to ship.

By the time I received my *Esquire* assignment, several small companies were making add-on equipment for the Altair. A number of others were even beginning to sell copies posing as competing machines. A few, very few, staunch individuals were starting to write some crude software to show and swap with friends. The classic of the period was probably Steve Dompier's rendition, for the Altair, of "Daisy," the same song that in 1957 had become the first melodic refrain ever to be uttered by a computer.

The Altair had no ability to produce sound of any kind. It certainly could not play music. What Dompier had done was to so program the machine that the static it generated produced a scratchy facsimile of the tune on a nearby radio.

The add-on equipment being made for the Altair was a near necessity for its owners, since the rudimentary computer kit itself lacked some of the basic amenities associated with personal computing today. For example, it had no keyboard. Data was entered by flicking a series of thirty-two switches up and down.

At this stage, personal computing was so confusing a task that very few people managed ever to do anything definitive with their machines. They just worked at it. In fact, they counted themselves lucky if they could get their computer put together.

Suppose you were one of the few whose computers were up and running. In other words, not only had you managed to assemble the whole kit, but it was actually functional. Suppose you had even purchased, as an optional extra, a video display module, so you could see what was happening as you worked. The television set, for that's all a display module was in those early days, allowed you to view the results of your labors on screen instead of merely watching the computer's red panel lights go on and off.

Suppose, too, you had loaded into your machine a computer language called BASIC, which Bill Gates, later to found Microsoft, had modified especially for the new Altair. This you had done with the aid of a tape cassette recorder, also an optional item, attached to the back of the computer by means of a long cable. The plug hadn't fit—another tradition carried over to present-day personal computer outfitting. However, after several hours on the phone to the manufacturer and a visit to the local Radio Shack for parts, you had managed to induce the computer to listen to the tape. With BASIC in its temporary memory, your machine was ready to understand whatever you might enter in that language.

Let's say you were going to write the title of this book, so you wanted to enter the letter *T*. Looking at the eight switches lined up along the bottom of the computer, you set them as follows: one up, the next two down, one more up, then three down, and the last one up. When you flicked another switch set off to the side, the letter was entered, and *T* appeared on the screen. On to the *H*. Two switches up. . . . Gutenberg could have done the job nine times faster.

Actually, it was even more complicated, but you get the idea. The point, however, is that it was possible, and the possibilities, however ill-defined as yet, were what seemed to have captured the imagination of those with whom I talked in my pursuit of a home computer story. Vague but wondrous future feats were apparently in store for the tiny blinking-eyed machine, though no one could tell me in more than the dreamiest terms what they were.

Among the early prophets of microcomputerdom, besides Processor Technology's Lee Felsenstein, were Bill and Louise Etra, whose New York loft was a cross between an electronically amplified shrine to the martial arts and a video vision of the European Renaissance. Bill wanted to synthesize video images. Louise wanted to synthesize art. Both wanted to convince me that an aesthetic revolution, one which, frankly, I contemplated with aversion, was in the making.

Then there was Avery Johnson, who, with a doctorate in electrical engineering from MIT and five years of postgraduate study in neurology, had been leading a *Mother Earth News*, back-to-the-land existence in the country. Having traded his chickens in for a Prime computer, a minicomputer much larger and more powerful than any micro would be for a decade, Avery was now prognosticating a future peopled with computer-aided haptic reflex loops wherein, when you touched a machine, it actually "touched" you back.

"Nowhere between lovers," Avery pointed out, "can you pass your mathematical plane and say, 'Here, see? This message is going this way and that one the other way.'"

Avery's dream was to add "Telegrasp" to the evolving personal computer. His intention was not to create carnal computers, but to put the abstract capabilities of electronic circuitry to a more intimate social use. Shoebox-sized enclosures filled with inflated bags and sensors could be attached to the machines, in turn interconnected by Ma Bell. One could then stick one's hands into one's own box and "feel," through the telephone lines, other hands inserted in another box thousands of miles away.

Technically, what was involved in Avery's Telegrasp was a principle called a self-organizing controller, SOC for short, an electronic equivalent of biofeedback whereby a device constantly adjusts its configuration in response to outside stimuli. SOCs had already been applied to controlling industrial production in chemical factories, where the temperature of a mixing vat, say, must constantly be adjusted to take into account changes in temperature caused by the chemical reaction itself. On a smaller scale, the principle was theoretically applicable to the home. Greenhouses and other enclosed surroundings where environmental changes occur and should be regulated could all be managed by a SOC.

Control was a big dream in the heady, early days of personal computing. So was telephone communications in general, and that aspect of it involving computers in particular.

The first personal computer modem, the device allowing one microcomputer to deal with another, or with a big brother, by phone, had yet to be invented. Nevertheless, telephone phreaks, as they spelled it, were very much in evidence on the computer scene. Stephen Wozniak started out building blue boxes, those electronic devices used to access telephone lines illegally, and ended up a few years later as co-founder of Apple Computer, Inc., and designer of its first micro. Another phreak, Robert Osband, convinced me that, technologically, at least, computers and telephones were as natural a combination as horses and carriages, and much faster, though in many cases less legal.

Then there was John Draper, who became known far and wide as Captain Crunch, after his favorite cereal. Each box of the cereal contained a whistle. Draper's contribution to the promotion of breakfast foods was his discovery that blowing the whistle into the mouthpiece of a telephone generated the precise 2,600-cycle tone controlling the release circuitry of the long-distance trunk lines. Given this whistle and a little expertise, one could call anywhere in the world for free. Incarcerated for his compulsive use of this discovery, Draper spent his time in retreat authoring the respectable word processing program EasyWriter.

Recently, I noticed that AT&T, in what must be an amazing oversight on the part of its advertising department, has been using Cap'n Crunch—the original breakfast version, that is—in its corporate advertisements. Truth to tell, it would not surprise me to see Draper himself appearing next in the company ads, promoting its personal computer.

A disparate fringe group of technointellectuals, the early computer enthusiasts evidenced a single-mindedness far beyond anything I'd ever seen before. If their vision of the future was no less hazy than that of the rest of us, one thing was certain: Utopia would be digital.

Perhaps the individual who best epitomized the madcap thrust toward a symbiotic relation between man and machine was Ted Nelson. No one could take Nelson altogether seriously. On the other hand, somehow one had to.

Ted Nelson, who even then had established himself as the perennial enfant terrible of personal computing, had just published *Computer Lib!*, a volume of computer futurism in the oversize format and crammed-full style of the *Whole Earth Catalog*. The current *Whole Earth Software Catalog* is a pale, commercial, limited, Yuppie shadow of the original counter-culture reference work.

Computer Lib! was a pyrotechny of ideas, some impractical, some inevitable. It contained the rantings of a madman, the vision of a prophet, and the incoherent babblings of a future that was being pulled into the present by the sheer will of one man. An underground best-seller now mostly mildewing in oblivion, *Computer Lib!* was the one book every personal computing pioneer in the mid-seventies had lying on the floor along with half a dozen recent issues of *Byte*.

Sinking back in my bath, waiting for all the disparate pieces of information and innuendo I had gleaned on personal computing to fall into place for my article as they usually did, given enough time, I thumbed through a copy of *Byte*, the bible of the computer cult, once more.

Incomprehensible! There was no other word for it. One could plow through whole sentences containing not a whit of concession to grammar, style, or form. Granted, the magazine was a new publication, put out by a group of computer hobbyists up in the ski country of New England. But hardly any of the words were English, and the smeary pictures with their ghoulish color tones gave the impression of cubism put through a blender.

Still, from everything I'd heard, there had to be something in the magazine. Obviously the fault must lie not in the unintelligibility of *Byte*, but in my lack of comprehension. Apparently, I wasn't really going to see any further into this curious future without taking up the digital gauntlet.

Well, so be it. But then maybe I could at least choose my own gauntlet. Grabbing a towel and still clutching *Byte*, I stepped out of the bath and headed for the telephone. Calling the magazine's office despite the latish hour, I asked for Virginia Peschke, the publisher. During the fifteen-minute conversation that ensued, I outlined the idea just forming in my mind, a plan for a magazine aimed at the first-time computerist, someone whose closest previous contact with the machines had been those punch cards the telephone company enclosed with its bill.

Virginia laughed. No one who wasn't already crazy about computers would have any interest in a magazine on the subject. Besides, she opined, there were two reasons why people bought *Byte*. The first was so that they could carry the magazine around, cover out, to show how with-it they were. The second was so that they could read the ads. The editorial matter made no difference.

As a writer, I took immediate affront to that notion. Once I became a publisher, it didn't take me long to realize how astute she had been.

Nevertheless, after ten years or so of eating oatmeal and rice and chicken hearts while collecting rejection slips from publishers as a struggling young writer in New York, one develops a certain disdain for their opinions. The feeling tends to persist even when publishers and editors begin responding to proffered manuscripts with small checks instead of rejection slips. In fact, I found vestiges of it persisting long after I'd had half a dozen books and innumerable articles in print, and had moved my family to a farm a long way from the tiny, one-room Manhattan apartment Susan and I had in black humor wallpapered with the rejection slips.

It was with a steadfast belief in the interest and influence of the written word that I decided to convince the aficionados I had encountered in my wanderings through the silicon streets to explain what was happening to all the other curious novices out there like me—by writing for a beginner's computer magazine. I chose the name *ROM: Computer Applications for Living* for it. After all, considering the sheer amount of drive, enthusiasm, and intensity I'd seen pulsating through the individuals involved in this new technology, there had to be *some* worthwhile applications for personal computers.

One of the advantages of being a writer is that one can detour in life in almost any direction that arouses one's curiosity. Thus it was that I found myself swept up in a bit of the future completely unrelated to my past—a technoklutz in computerland.

2: Countdown to Tomorrow

It doesn't take a computer to start a magazine, even one devoted to the beasts. In the case of Susan and myself, the sole and joint venture capitalists for my bathtub-born publishing enterprise, it was mostly a matter of taking out a second and a third and a fourth mortgage on the house, converting the tractor barn into an office, and persuading could-be writers to apply their posteriors to a chair long enough to turn out a manuscript.

We did, however, in deference to the budding advantages of electronification, purchase a Compugraphic, a computerized typesetting machine, and contract with a fulfillment house, which uses computers, to crank out the mailing lists that not only regularly address issues of magazines to their rightful subscribers, but also put each recipient on every other mailing list that might be remotely connected with the periodical's field of inquiry. The subject of our proposed publication being more or less computers, we were soon to find ourselves in the same direct-mail cubbyhole with meet-your-mate organizations and vendors of atmospheric air purifiers aimed at promoting a healthier environment for man and machine.

With a rudimentary organization in place and a masthead featuring Susan and myself under various pseudonyms to flesh out a meager staff of two full-time co-workers and a part-time one, the magazine was ready to roll. I set off for the First West Coast Computer Faire in San Francisco to look for advertisers and to promote *ROM*, my suitcase full of flyers.

Organized by Jim Warren, editor of the classic, if incomprehensible to all but the few, *Dr. Dobb's Journal of Computer Calisthenics and Orthodontia*, the barely publicized hobbyist show held at San Francisco's Civic Center in April of 1977 blossomed into an international event with 12,755 attendees, including a tour group from, naturally, Japan. A joyous circuit circus, it was to the electronics buff what Woodstock had been to the hippie of the sixties, both an exhilarating event and one whose pinnacle could never be reached again.

My first glimpse of the exhibit hall was from the second-floor balcony, beneath which spread out a relatively deserted grid of booths divided by yellow curtains, each cubicle filled with the wares of the new technology. Then the doors opened and the five lines of eager enthusiasts encircling the Civic Center began streaming in, flooding the hall with the spirit of Jim Warren's slogan, "Computer Power for the People." Later on, small groups of people would cluster here and there in the balcony, forming knots of humanity along the vast expanse of bleachers to exchange ideas and information and to make deals. From those deals would be fashioned companies constituting the early underpinnings of the personal computer industry.

Descending from my lookout and wading through the rows and rows of exhibits, I decided that Warren's choice of the ersatz Middle English spelling "Faire" for his venture had been quite astute. A carnival atmosphere prevailed, for, like the old trade fairs where the wheels of commerce first began

15

to turn, this meeting was a celebration as well as a gathering for the exchange of wares. As in that different age, too, there were plenty of horse traders in evidence.

Among the T-shirts imprinted with computerific slogans and the biorhythm charts from the IMSAI computer company, people of all ages could be found playing Star Trek, Target, and Computer Billiards. The games, so far still the central answer to my question, "What can you do with a personal computer?," were in black and white. But a rainbow was on its way.

On a giant Advent projection screen used as a monitor, Apple displayed a constantly changing pattern of computer-generated colors. Elsewhere, ALF Products played its music machine, a polymorphous laser-beam video show cast a would-be spell over the audience, and Midwest Scientific's magic wand read bar codes like those now found on every piece of merchandise in so many retail stores.

More important as an indicator of where personal computing was heading in the second year of its infancy was another, even more startling innovation: keyboards. The Sol, Processor Technology's computer so notably sandwiched in its hand-rubbed walnut case (left over from a failed stereo manufacturing venture), was replete with its own keyboard. The Apple II, the first commercial Apple, had one. So did the Commodore PET, another recent arrival on the microcomputer scene. Older computers, such as the Altair, the IMSAI, and TDL's Xitan, machines from a previous generation all of six months or so before, seemed doomed to ignominy by failing to provide a keyboard.

Alphanumeric keyboards, of course, go back well before the invention of digital computers, to 1868, in fact. While Johannes Brahms was incorporating calls from the Alpine horns of Zurich into his First Symphony, the less-remembered Christopher Latham Sholes was composing Qwerty. Brahms was probably little concerned with the fingering required of musicians to perform his symphony. To Sholes, fingering was crucial. On his primitive typewriter, the consecutive striking of adjacent keys would often snare their wobbly linkages. Therefore, letters frequently combined in

16

English had to be separated on the keyboard by others less often used.

Efficiency experts have long railed against the calculated slowness and awkwardness of the Qwerty keyboard, named for the first six top-row keys. Nevertheless, despite the electronic speed and other marvels that personal computers have come to offer, the mundane fact remains that the principal way to enter information into and operate these machines remains the same old typewriter keyboard that attached itself to them around the time of that fateful Faire.

True, a whole new generation of software now manipulates cursors on screens by using mice, those palm-sized, button-eared plastic rodents only recently ushered into the computer arena. Move the mouse on your desk, and the mouse sends a signal up its tail, causing the cursor to make a matching move on the video monitor. Press an ear button, and you can "pick up" a block of text and position it elsewhere on the screen. All the same, entering actual, new data remains the province of the keyboard.

As for those marvelous voice-activated computer systems that enable you to give your machine dictation or tell it what you want done and have your spoken request promptly carried out, their time may come. But the full development of voice recognition is, in my opinion, at least five years away, and more likely ten or twenty or more. Till then, it's the keyboard or nothing for most of us when it comes to making a computer jump through its hoops.

Despite this fact, there exists no such thing as a standardized keyboard, except for the Qwerty layout, in the still fragmented, "That's not the way we do it here" world of computing. Choosing the keyboard that is best for you may be one of the most important decisions you make in acquiring your computer equipment, along with selecting the software that comes closest to doing what you want done and finding the hardware that will run it.

But, you wonder, doesn't a computer nowadays come complete with a keyboard? Well, yes, it does. But that doesn't mean you have to live with it. A classic case in point is the IBM PC. For some unaccountable reason, IBM, the company

17

that set the standard for the typewriter industry with its popular Selectric keyboard, chose not to use the same layout for its computers. A lot of people have objected to the PC's placement of the tab and return keys further out to the sides than their position on a normal keyboard. So widespread has the dissatisfaction been that one company, Key Tronic, catering to those who would rather switch than fight, has built up a sizable business manufacturing replacement keyboards for the PC designed along more traditional lines. Special keyboards are being similarly manufactured for most popular computers.

On the avant-garde front, a number of keyboards incorporating the Dvorak layout, a configuration that makes typing much faster and less tiring, are making their way to market. These are of special interest to those who are just beginning their search for a computer and who have not spent much time at a keyboard lately. Some computer keyboards, such as that of the Apple IIc, can be converted to the Dvorak layout at the flick of a switch and the moving of the labeled keycaps to match.

Even if your mind has had Qwerty imprinted since day one, it may pay to switch to Dvorak. The reeducation process often takes less than a week with a computer tutorial, and the benefits, its advocates claim, last a lifetime. The availability of a Dvorak keyboard may well become a crucial deciding factor in future choices where computers are concerned. Then again, Esperanto has been around for a hundred years without making a major impact.

When you are comparing keyboards, the first thing to look for is comfort—in all its aspects, from the ease with which you can move the unit around, even placing it in your lap if you so desire, to the feel of the keys themselves. Stiff, unresponsive keys, mushy ones, and those that seem to wobble and rattle, distracting you as you attempt to concentrate on your task, can all lead to unnecessary errors and fatigue.

Try to spend at least one uninterrupted hour at the keyboard before you buy a computer. Your typing, or keyboarding, as computerists call it, is all-important, and it is surprising how your finger response can change over such a

18

relatively short period of time as an hour. A keyboard that seems just right when you first start typing may well turn out to be on the soft side once you have pecked away for a while. A soft keyboard leads to numerous repeat errors, such as "The quick brown fox" unaccountably becoming "Thhe quiiick brrown foxx."

(An interesting sidelight on how we react to electronics technology can be gleaned by watching yourself when you hold down a key in order to underline or perform some other repeat function. If you are like me and most people, you will subconsciously press harder and harder, trying to speed up the stream of characters. This is a carryover from the mechanical mentality, wherein force, more than time, is associated with producing results.)

Beyond the general feel of the keyboard and the standard alphanumeric layout lies the realm of numeric keypads and special function keys not normally found on a typewriter. A separate numeric keypad with an arrangement like that of a calculator simplifies the entry of figures for accounting and similar applications, though it is possible to use your computer for bookkeeping and financial analysis by entering data through the standard typewriter number keys.

Cursor control keys, which permit you to move the cursor up, down, right, and left on the video screen, are essential even if you have a mouse to run these errands too. The absence of cursor keys on Apple's Macintosh computer, mouse or no mouse, is a drawback for most people.

The arrangement of the cursor keys in the pattern of a compass rose is much preferable to their layout in a simple row. A so-called home key, best located in the center of the rose, allows you to move the cursor with a single keystroke from anywhere on the screen to the top left-hand corner. It is a practical timesaver, though not an absolute necessity.

There are a number of special, dedicated (or single-purpose) keys that are particularly useful for word processing and other tasks involving switching back and forth within the data on which you are working. Previous-screen and next-screen keys permit you to page through an electronic manuscript at the press of a button. A delete key enables you to erase any character on which the cursor is resting and pulls the rest of the line leftward to fill the void.

Such specialized keys as escape and control, used for multistep functions, are standard on all personal computer keyboards. You will become familiar with them soon after you plug in one of these machines. However, the more versatile programmable function keys, usually labeled F1, F2, and so on, may or may not be available on a particular computer. In general, because they abbreviate the steps in a task, the more programmable keys the better. The standard number is ten.

Programmable function keys allow you, or rather the software you run, to assign to each such key whatever task is deemed necessary, allowing frequently used commands to be reduced to a single keystroke. For example, pressing F6 while running the word processing software PeachText will induce the computer to scan the entire manuscript and automatically substitute one designated word for another—say the name "Sue" for "Susan"—or complete any other search-and-replace function you might wish to perform. All in all, programmable function keys save you an awful lot of time—which, after all, is what computing is supposed to be all about.

To the devotees at that first computer Faire, however, such sophisticated choices were not available. Simply having a keyboard was enough. Indeed, some of the manufacturers surviving the early years have retained that feeling to this day. Apple, for instance, never added function keys to its tremendously popular Apple II series. With the Macintosh and its predilection for mouse-powered software, in fact, the company is attempting to return even the keyboard to the hinterland of specialized tasks, such as word processing. Some find this approach a fantastic step forward, others feel it is a giant step backward. Only time will tell how users will vote with their pocketbooks.

Technology surprisingly often refuses to cast millstones from about its neck. The old Qwerty keyboard is one instance of this doggedness. Another is the tape cassette still being sold as the medium of program storage for a number of the less expensive home computers, such as the Adam.

20

In the ancient days of the mid-seventies when personal computers first began to emerge from the primordial electronic swamps of Silicon Valley, one of the numerous enigmas of their evolution was the form their external memory, the computer's equivalent of your library or record collection, would take. Eventually there arose two predominant types, cassette tapes and disks, and those two forms still prevail today. Which you choose will greatly affect the usability of your personal computer for a long time to come.

The computer's library, or external memory, is indefinitely expandable with either storage medium. But cassette tape storage requires your computer to skim the whole of a tape, or volume, so to speak, in order to find the information for which it is searching. It's like looking up, say, gum arabic in a book on industrial gums and leafing all the way from page 1 to page 322 before finding it. The next bit of information you need might turn out to be on page 3, and you would have turned all those pages back again one by one before locating it. Cassettes cannot utilize an index.

Put a disk into a computer's drive, on the other hand, and the machine can look up information anywhere it wants, simply by referring to the disk index and going directly to the spot indicated. It's like flipping open that book on industrial gums right to page 322 because the index tells you that's where the information on gum arabic is located.

You will still find computers at the low end of the price scale, machines such as Coleco's Adam and the Atari series, using peanut-butter-proof ROM cartridges, the acronym in this case referring to read-only memory rather than its namesake magazine. As one might infer from the term, a ROM cartridge's utility is limited to what has been prestored in the cartridge; what, in other words, the computer can read. Because they can't be damaged readily, and because their contents can be read quickly by a computer, ROM cartridges are good memory devices for games and for young children. They also allow a computer to load their contents much more quickly than disks do, which could be a great asset in business computing. But for some inexplicable reason, perhaps their association with games, manufacturers of the more ex-

21

pensive personal computers never incorporate a cartridge slot in their machines, and no business software is available on this medium. The current exception is the IBM PCjr, which does have cartridge slots and for which Lotus 1-2-3 is available in cartridge form.

The limitations of ROM cartridges become evident when you want to store new information, be it a program you have created, data on your investment portfolio, or some computer graphics you have executed. You can't store anything on a cartridge. So here you must choose between cassettes and disks.

At the time of the First West Coast Computer Faire, your only choice for any kind of external memory was the cassette. Though available for large computers at a cost of thousands of dollars, disk drives for personal computers were virtually nonexistent. Processor Technology was in the midst of developing one for its Sol computer. Called the Helios, it was roughly the size of a single-drawer file cabinet, or four times the size of the computer itself. Stephen Wozniak, the engineering genius behind the Apple, was also working on a disk drive, a highly compact unit that went on display at the Second West Coast Computer Faire in March of 1978.

Still, another year was to pass before disk drives would make an appreciable mark in the personal computer marketplace. When they finally did so, Wozniak's elegant version helped immensely in driving Apple to success.

Today, as in 1977, there are no truly viable alternatives in external memory devices. But whereas in those early days the sole practical option was cassette tape storage, now the only way to remember, if you are a personal computer, is by way of disks. While cassette drives remain available for a number of personal computers, including the Commodore line and Coleco's Adam, for which the company introduced a high-speed tape drive called the Digital Data Pack, buying a cassette drive in this day and age is unequivocally a mistake.

If that's the case, you may well ask, how come cassette drives are still being sold? Therein lies a tale of dollars and sense.

Personal computing is not an inexpensive hobby. As anyone who has become involved in the field will tell you, the computer itself may seem relatively expensive, but your checkbook hasn't seen anything until it is called upon to cover the care and feeding of the machine. Particularly costly is the computer's insatiable appetite for programs, at $30, $50, or even $500 apiece. Worse yet, a $200 or $300 computer calling for a $400 disk drive just doesn't seem to make any sense at all. Why should one pay more for a peripheral than for the machine itself? Enter the $80 cassette drive—though not in your case, let's hope.

Interestingly enough, comparative reliability, which is one of the criteria contributing to the popularity of cassettes among audiophiles, is one of the very criteria by which they should be ruled a poor choice for computers. Music enthusiasts might be less than happy with cassettes' occasional habit of chewing up tape in a drive. Nevertheless, for their purposes, these recording devices are dependable, provide easy storage, and don't scratch the way records do. In the case of a computer, however, cassettes are anything but reliable.

All too often, when cassettes try to deal with the more precise digital data required in computing, they fail. For example, when you try to load a program or information stored on tape, it is not unusual for the computer simply to sit there expectantly, with nothing on its mind, because of a tape-induced error caused by stretching Mylar or a misaligned read-record head.

Furthermore, when a program does load, or boot, to use the jargon of the trade, it seems to take forever. Remember that cassette storage is slow, very slow. Waiting for your computer to search through hundreds of feet of tape for one bit of information and then hundreds more for the next is like waiting for Godot. It makes a joke of applications like word processing, unless you are dealing only with twenty-word memos. Cassette memory storage for the present generation of personal computers is about as appropriate a technology as powering a Porsche by hitching an ox to the front bumper.

Another drawback of cassettes as vehicles of external computer memory is that, compared to floppy disks, they simply don't hold very much information. Many of the programs you are apt to want to run will not fit on a cassette. This results in what is perhaps the most telling blow of all to cassette storage. A lot of software companies simply will not bother to put their products on tape. Now if you can't buy the software you want to run on your computer, what kind of a bargain have you got?

Their practical obsolescence notwithstanding, cassettes have about them a comforting aura of familiarity, and if there is one thing that is hard to come by in the confusing world of computers, it's familiarity. Thus the novice may be sorely tempted to buy a cassette drive, even if it represents yesterday's technology.

Although I expect to see cassette drives and cassette programs being sold for at least another year or so—probably at well-nigh-irresistible low prices—you should resist anyhow. About the only people who will be purchasing these Edsels of memory will be first-time buyers looking for a bargain— which, considering what you can do with them, cassettes are not. Getting all tangled up in tape is no way to start out in personal computing. There are enough other problems to conquer.

If you are uncomfortable with the idea of floppy disks as the realistic alternative to tapes, try to think of them as merely specialized records. Floppy disks, so named because they are indeed soft and floppy, are housed in stiff plastic envelopes or, in the case of the newer and smaller microfloppies, cartridges. Their jackets are never removed by the user.

You can see part of an actual floppy disk through the oblong access hole in its protective envelope, the aperture through which the disk drive's read-write head performs its task. All that is normally observable, however, is the unbroken matte gray surface itself, two shades darker than battleship gray. The magical secrets lying hidden on this metallic oxide surface, like so many of the computer's own internal mysteries, can be visualized only by your mind's eye.

Because of their protective coat, floppy disks look square instead of round like phonograph records. Instead of putting one of these "records" on a turntable and watching the tone arm drop down and start tracking, you flip the disk into the slit of a disk drive, close the latch, and watch a red light go on. The unseen disk drive head, which, as it happens, resembles that of a tape recorder, then begins to read whatever is stored on the disk.

Unless you want to look at the world from an engineer's point of view, that's all you really need to know about disks in order to run them, except, of course, that the disk you use must be compatible with your computer's disk drive. Then again, you wouldn't try to play a 33-rpm record on an old portable phonograph that accepts only 45s, if you could even find one.

The playing speed is not the only difference between a 33-rpm and a 45-rpm record. The size is different, too. Likewise, personal computers started out with eight-inch disks as their standard. But smaller five-and-a-quarter-inch disks called minifloppies were also available, and when Wozniak designed the Apple's disk drive around them, they speedily became the industry standard. Newer three-and-a-half-inch disks, designated microfloppies, pioneered by Sony, are being utilized by such companies as Hewlett-Packard in its 110 portable and Apple in its heavily advertised Macintosh.

Memory marches on. As in all things having to do with computers, today's standard may be obsolete tomorrow, and tomorrow may dawn precipitately. But in the case of disks, if their eventual size is still in question, their present usefulness is not.

Tanya, our middle child, pack rat, and junior computer cognoscente, collects disks as if they were bubble-gum cards. Piles of them, waiting to be used, lie scattered about here and there in what was once a tractor shed, became *ROM* magazine's art department, and now has undergone one more metamorphosis into a computer room. Their order is on a par with that reigning in her closet. Though she can find what she wants, none of the rest of us can.

Like that disk-littered computer room and Tanya's closet, the order and organization of a disk itself are hidden to the eyes of the beholder. When you buy software on disk, its orderly structure is part and parcel of your purchase. The program is ready to run as soon as you put the disk into your

25

computer's drive. (That's assuming, of course, that you have purchased software compatible with your machine. The Apple version of Bank Street Writer, for instance, will not run on the Atari, and vice versa.)

When you buy blank diskettes, on the other hand, for use in recording the results of your word processing or other computerized tasks, you will have to format, or initialize, them before they can be utilized. A blank diskette is just that, as empty as one of those write-it-yourself books so popular these days.

The job of initializing the disk is actually performed by your computer, following the instructions of its disk operating system, or DOS. The reason this industrious software is referred to as a disk operating system is that so much of its work involves the disk and how information is stored on it.

In formatting, the computer sets up an information matrix, or map, to define for itself where on the disk specific details will be stored and may be found. It delineates the number of "pages" the disk should have in order to accommodate its particular internal design. Most personal computers divide their disks into from thirty-five to eighty such pages laid out in magnetized concentric rings called tracks. Then they magnetically slice the whole disk into from ten to sixteen pie-shaped wedges called sectors, which are roughly the equivalent of paragraphs on a page.

In the case of the so-called hard-sectored disks, not much used any more, the pie was, literally, physically cut when the disk was manufactured. On a ten-sector disk, for example, ten holes were spaced evenly around the disk. An eleventh hole punched in between two of the others served as a rotational index. Without this index hole, a computer could not sense which part of the disk it was dealing with.

Hard-sector disks used a photodetector to locate the sector holes. Their flexibility was limited by this mechanical dependency, and they were fairly crude. But they were inexpensive.

As is wont to happen in electronics, however, the disk controllers that performed the same function magnetically declined rapidly in price as the personal computer revolution exploded. Now personal computers use the more versatile and dependable soft-sector disks almost exclusively.

Soft-sector disks still have one physical hole, the one defining sector 01, the first slice of the pie. Turn a diskette slowly in its envelope, touching only the edges of the large center hole, and eventually you will be able to see this index hole through the small, round, paper-punch-hole-sized access aperture in the disk's protective jacket. The larger oval window in the jacket exposes the disk a little at a time so the disk drive can read and write information to and from the disk.

A third hole in the protective jacket, a small notch on the outside edge, is called a write protect notch. As long as it is left uncovered, the disk drive can sense the notch, and new information can be written onto the disk. If you wish to protect whatever information you have stored on the disk, you can cover this notch with one of the little adhesive tabs included in a new package of blank disks. With the write protect tab in place, the disk drive can only read information from the disk, not write to it. Thus the tab keeps the disk drive from accidentally covering up information previously stored on the disk.

Your role in disk formatting is simply one of supply and demand, so to speak. You provide the disks, make sure there are no write protect tabs in place, and request the computer to initialize them for you. Your machine does the rest. In the case of the Tandy 2000, for instance, all you do is type the instruction FORMAT. The computer responds with the screen message, "Insert new diskette for drive A: and strike any key when ready." Your doing so initiates the formatting process. The screen then displays the message, "Formatting tracks," along with a small line of dashes. Each dash represents one track to be laid down. As this track is electronically defined on your blank disk, the dash is replaced by a period. If a flaw is detected on the disk and the track where it is located cannot be used, a question mark appears instead of a period. This does not mean that the disk itself cannot be used. The formatting procedure of DOS automatically locks out bad sectors, so your computer will not try to store information on these tracks. By the same token, however, a disk so tagged

27

will not be capable of holding as much information as an unflawed one.

Once a disk has been formatted, it is ready to be used for information storage. Where on the disk what information is deposited will be controlled by the disk operating system. As the disk rotates, at five revolutions per second, the read-write head slides back and forth across the area exposed by the oval window in the protective sleeve, either reading data from or writing it into the individual sectors of each track. Where it puts what information is up to DOS. You won't have to find it again. DOS will. Your concern is with how much memory capacity each disk has.

The greater a disk's storage capacity, the less often you will have to put in a new one, which is why double-sided disks were developed, giving a 100 percent increase in storage capacity without requiring any fancy new technology. Switching disks sounds, and is, as easy as loading a toaster. Nevertheless, it is time consuming, and the need for it always seems to arise at the most inconvenient juncture.

A more spectacular increase in storage capacity is provided by double-density disks and quad-density disks, as they are known. These superstorage disks are being used by more and more machines. Their unassuming names notwithstanding, they can hold as much as five to ten times the information single-density disks do.

Because these disks are so crammed with data, they require an extremely precisely engineered tool to retrieve that information. They are reminiscent of the two-volume edition of the unabridged *Oxford English Dictionary;* you need a magnifying lens in order to read the entries. Your computer, in other words, must be equipped with a double- or a quad-density disk drive.

Hard disks store information even more compactly. They are to floppies of any density what a Turkish miniature is to a Jackson Pollock canvas. Only the most expensive, top-of-the-line personal computers come equipped with these amazing devices. However, acquiring one of them does not necessarily entail buying a new machine if you already own a computer. These somewhat expensive but highly useful peripherals are available as add-ons for almost every personal computer made, from the Apple, IBM, Kaypro, old Osborne, and Tandy Radio Shack machines to the low-priced Atari and Commodore. Personally, though, I would probably draw the line at outfitting an economy model like an Atari or a Commodore with a hard disk. Something in the back of my mind keeps nagging that it doesn't make sense to buy a $1500-plus peripheral for a $200 computer.

The true measure of need for a hard disk, however, lies not so much in its comparative cost as in how often you find yourself switching disks when running your computer. The value of a hard disk lies in its speed of operation and its capacity. Once you have become used to these features, you will never want to give them up.

Everything I have written over the past year is contained on the single hard disk of an IBM PC/XT. Lest you think I have been shirking my work, the ten-megabyte disk will hold the equivalent of around 2,500 typed pages, roughly the storage capacity of thirty floppies for the same machine. Anything on the disk can be called up for a fast review, one of the features that really separates word processing from typing. I can locate a story and have it on screen in less than a minute instead of having to plow through half-a-dozen file cabinets of old articles as I once had to do.

A book-length "manuscript" that would fill two floppies occupies only a small portion of a hard disk. Thus even lengthy works do not entail disk switching during review or revision. A mere two floppies to be shifted back and forth may not seem a significant problem at first glance. But one of the basic laws of word processing the salesman never mentions, unless he happens to be peddling hard disks, is that the paragraph you are searching for is always on the other floppy.

For applications like large business budgets, data bases, and mailing lists with a couple thousand entries, the time saved by not having to switch disks becomes quite significant. Instead of waiting a number of seconds for the required data to be transferred from one floppy to the computer's memory, then inserting the next disk and repeating the operation, and

29

the wait, and so on until the several disks of your data base or financial listings are read, you can measure the speed of access to all your data mostly in milliseconds.

The new integrated software packages which combine the functions of several separate programs, such as spreadsheet, data base, word processing, and communications, all interactive, are much facilitated by having a single source of data. Some of the newest integrated programs, such as Symphony, require so much archival memory that they are virtually ineffective unless used in conjunction with a hard disk.

Even if you don't really need its larger storage capacity for data at the moment, a hard disk still offers one unbeatable advantage over its floppy counterpart: you can keep all your programs on one disk. I have more than twenty frequently used programs on my hard disk. Because of the computer's ready access to them, I can switch almost instantly from word processing to a spreadsheet, a spelling checker, a calculator, an outliner, checkwriting software, or any other program I might need, all with one or two simple commands, and all without inserting a single disk—well, almost.

Some software, because of its copy protection scheme, allows only part of a program to be transferred to hard disk, still requiring you to insert a floppy when you run it. However, even when using such software, you are saved a lot of disk switching, and I think most of these copy protection schemes will be revised in the near future so that the programs they restrain can be loaded completely onto hard disk. The marketplace will demand it. As the price of hard disks continues to decline, and as the convenience of using them becomes increasingly well known, people simply aren't going to put up with flipping floppies anymore.

All the considerations of memory lead steadfastly to a basic rule of thumb: more is definitely better. So when you buy a computer, don't skimp on the bookshelves. Buy the model with both the most internal memory, the brain size of the machine itself, as it were, and the most disk storage capacity you can afford, even if it means waiting a while to purchase some of the extras you may want, such as a printer or a communications modem. For without enough memory to do the job, you can't run a lot of the software available. And without software, you have a large paperweight, not a computer.

Such modern-day marvels as hard disks and automatic formatting were mere glimmers in the eyes of the exhibitors at that first let-'em-loose-in-a-candy-store West Coast Computer Faire. Mostly there was a lot of talk about the "significant" things personal computers would be able to do. There were dreams—or nightmares, depending on how you viewed them —of the computer having dinner cooking when you came home from work, protecting you from burglars, maximizing the efficiency of your hot water heater by, among other things, turning on the dishwasher after midnight when the electricity rates were lowest and, in short, doing everything in the home but the windows.

Games, however, were still the driving force behind personal computing. At the close of the Faire, as Jim Warren's public-address-system-amplified jubilance rang through the hall, Ted Nelson broke in with, "This is Captain Kirk. Prepare for a blastoff." And personal computing did. All you needed to book a flight was a computer of your own.

3: The Joy of Frustration; or, An Electronic Fly in the Circuits

I t was an unusually cold, stormy day in May when the UPS man drove up the country lane leading to our farm. Unceremoniously he handed me a package the size of two shoeboxes. It was awfully light for a computer, I thought, scribbling the old Hancock on the receipt form. Nevertheless, since it came from Processor Technology, it had to be the Sol. While at the Faire, I had arranged to procure a machine. After all, if I was going to run a computer magazine, what better way to find out what all the fuss was about than by having a bona fide representative of the subject matter around? In 1977, that usually meant assembling one yourself from a kit.

I took the package inside and looked for a knife. Three quick slashes across the strapping tape opened the box, exposing a bag full of electronics parts and a green instruction manual. It seemed the 8K memory module had arrived. The computer itself must still be somewhere in transit.

Stirring up a few charred logs in the fireplace to keep the chill away, I pulled a chair closer to the grate and turned to the first page of the manual, entitled, inspiringly enough, *8KRAM Static Read/Write Memory Module Assembly and Test Instructions.* For someone whose only previous contact with electricity had come from such tasks as rewiring an old electric stove in such a fashion that it blew either fuses or the frypan right off the top burner, the days to follow promised to prove quite an experience.

That first evening, I contented myself with trying to read the manual, several times. I supposed it might make sense to wait for the computer itself to arrive before actually starting the assembly project. In the end, however, I could restrain myself no longer. Any way one looked at it, I told myself, the computer was going to need memory.

The manual being replete with warnings about static electricity and synthetic fiber clothes, I decided to run right out first thing the following morning and buy some cotton shirts and underwear. An overreaction, no doubt. But since I had previously acquired the drip-dry habit, this seemed as good a time as any to break it. Susan, who really didn't have time for ironing, suggested I assemble the kit in my pajamas. The only time I had to work on the project was late at night, she pointed out, and the sleepwear was 100 percent cotton. I settled for 40 percent cotton and kept my shirt on.

Workshop fashions aside, the manual made clear that I would definitely need an ohmmeter, which my dictionary informed me was an instrument for measuring electrical resistance directly. The family electronics tool chest being limited so far to some twenty-amp fuses, some thirty-amp fuses, and some wirecutters that I had used to take down an electric fence on the west forty, I paid a visit to the local Radio Shack to pick up a super-duper-deluxe-model volt ohmmeter. It had more knobs on it than my stereo, but no doubt they would all accomplish something useful before the job was done.

While I was there, I also procured a more diminutive pair of wirecutters than those I already possessed, needle-nose pliers, and a twenty-five-watt soldering iron. In one spot the manual had suggested a controlled heat soldering iron, in another a plain twenty-five-watt version. The salesman assured me, I suspect because the controlled heat model was not in stock, that the regular one would do. I settled instead of selected.

Armed to the teeth, I returned home to tackle my project and answer the question, "Can the average Erik, equipped with little experience in the world of electronics beyond turning on a radio, assemble a computer kit?"

The answer looked like a good, solid "Well, maybe."

First among the preliminaries was the matter of determining whether all the hundreds of necessary parts were indeed there—not a simple task if one didn't even know what a diode looked like. Fortunately, there were pictures of the various components, which, cross-checked against the parts numbers, helped to make sense of them.

Initially there seemed to be a lot of missing pieces. By the third time I had gone over the checklist, however, I had found everything—well, almost everything. I still had only ten small resistors instead of the eleven specified. I also had some extra goodies. These ended up on the board anyhow, as it turned out. The manual had simply failed to mention them.

The failure of instructions accompanying the artifacts of personal computing to achieve the end for which they are presumably written is by now all but a well-established tradition. Actually, such procedural directives have never claimed to be actual instructions. Computerese has made mandatory all reference to them as documentation.

I suspect this usage traces its lineage to two sources. First of all, the manuals are usually so incomprehensible to the uninitiated that they cannot honestly be called instructive. Second, this written material accompanying both hardware and software items was first meant to document how the originator arrived at the product—so that the buyer could attempt to correct design mistakes and induce the product to work once purchased.

My introduction to this trial by consumer ordeal occurred when I called Processor Technology about that eleventh resistor I couldn't find in my memory kit. It appeared that the original plan had called for eleven resistors, the final kit had called for ten, and no one had taken the time to change the documentation to match the simplified design.

Matters of design and construction have improved greatly on the hardware front since the early days of kit computers. In software, on the other hand, you will still see a constant stream of revisions being issued. Hence the cryptic V1.1, V2.3, V3.1, and so on that you see stamped on software packages and disks.

V1.1, V1.2, V1.3, or a version thereabouts, is usually the first variation of a program to be released, the prior versions being unusable. In due course, after enough users have suffered the program's flaws and complained, the company makes corrections and additions, and the version number on the new copies shipped moves up a notch. This occurs a number of times until eventually, by the time version 3.1 or so is released, the software publisher is selling something that reasonably approximates what was promised in the first place. It is not only the technology of personal computing that is amazing, but its marketing as well. What other product is sold as the eighth wonder of the world—the promise to be fulfilled as soon as the customer figures out why it doesn't work so the publisher can fix it?

On the brighter side, at least today there is software available, and the computer comes assembled. Ordinarily you can get one up and running—if not necessarily doing what you want it to do—in less time than it took me to figure out what the various pieces of the Sol memory board were supposed to be.

I particularly remember coming across such unknowns as right-angle molex connectors and augat pins while sorting through the parts list. I had never met such animals before. Only through the process of elimination, assisted by a little telltale "MX" on the side of a brown doojiggy with right-angle protrusions and a matching thing to plug it into, was I finally able to assume with reasonable certainty that I had found the molex connector. That left only one part, a little row of pins. Augat pins, my dear Watson.

The checkoff and parts count for the Sol memory kit took about an hour. By the end of that time, I was anxious to start the actual assembly. I turned to the task with a sense of relief, thankful that the preliminaries were over at last.

Or so I thought. As it turned out, the board itself had to be checked for shorts before I could begin working on it. That meant unpacking my brand-new volt ohmmeter.

The instructions for the meter read, "Remove the case back and install the batteries." No mention was made of how the back was to be removed, nor was there anything on the meter itself to indicate the method. There were, however, three deeply recessed screws. I went for a Phillips screwdriver.

The front came off instead of the back. Nevertheless, the batteries fitted into place without difficulty. I zipped it all together again.

The next problem was that the needle did not rest on zero when the control switch was in the off position. For this situation there were remedial instructions. The needle was to be adjusted by means of the plastic screw located at the bottom of the meter face. That seemed simple enough—but a *plastic* screw? I went for a regular screwdriver.

Rummaging around in the household toolbox, I mused on how all the Radio Shack equipment seemed to be made in Korea, while the chips used by Processor Technology came from Singapore. Whatever had happened to the fabled American electronics industry?

With my meter's needle finally resting on zero, I began to test the circuit board. To do so, I had to figure out the proper setting for the volt ohmmeter. Obviously I was testing for some kind of movement of the needle. First I instinctively set the meter on the direct current side. Nothing happened. That was as it should be. But how did I know the meter knob was positioned properly?

Thinking about it for a minute, I reached the natural conclusion that I was testing for conductivity. When the probes were touched to a screwdriver, the needle refused to move.

Now even I know that a metal screwdriver conducts electricity, so obviously the dial must be in the wrong position. Turning the dial to various other points, I eventually ended up with the knob pointer on the low-scale side. The needle jumped. Maybe that was what I wanted? Sure enough, turning to the instructions again, I found a reference to "Using an ohmmeter on its lowest scale. . . ."

I had better read more carefully in the future.

My next task was to run through the eight-volt bus test and the five-volt bus test and the RAM area test. This is not to say that I had the slightest idea of what an eight-volt bus test and a five-volt bus test and a RAM test really were. I simply followed the instructions, quite blindly, to the letter. One way or another, I was going to have a computer.

Once I had discovered which pinholes to test, everything checked out. The board passed inspection. The rest was up to me.

Next, I was to install the heat sink. Now I admit the kit had looked as if it contained everything but, or perhaps including, the kitchen sink. Still, I was surprised to learn that the manufacturer would admit it. Checking my dictionary, I discovered that a heat sink collects heat from hot parts, keeping them from burning out. Clever.

The sink was supposed to sit on the board in such a way that the three wings of the triangular sink matched a triangle of mounting holes on the board. This should have been easy enough to arrange. Unfortunately, there was no discernible triangle on the board. With some protracted squinting, however, I could perceive a set of holes in the board that might be conceived of as a triangle. I so conceived of them.

Setting the screws, lock washers, and nuts required no more than three hands. There was at least $\frac{1}{32}$ of an inch between the heat-dissipating wings of the sink and the sides of the nuts.

The night I tackled the Sol memory board is etched in my memory, but I won't attempt a diode-by-diode description of the rest of the board's assembly. Suffice it to say that by the time our somewhat screwed-up rooster Oscar started crowing at three o'clock in the morning, I was the proud possessor of what appeared to be a working 8K memory board.

Today, procuring internal memory, the brains of the computer, is a lot easier, though not necessarily entirely painless. You won't have to learn to differentiate between capacitors and transistors or navigate a circuit board's curious map of component locations, featuring cryptic markers like D1, D3, R1, and U46, with a soldering iron, but you will have to be able to choose wisely among the many alternatives available. If you at least understand what machine memory is all about, your task will be simpler.

Memory is a curious thing. I remember sitting curled up, in the contorted fashion that only teenage limberness makes possible, much less comfortable, high above our back yard in the upper reaches of a catalpa tree, reading. Sometimes the wind would rock my leafy world to and fro, and occasionally I would reach for another sandwich or a glass of juice from the "icebox," a wooden milk crate jammed into the dividing branch beside me, as I eagerly turned the pages of *The Boy Mechanic* or one of those wonderful magazines of the day devoted to building one's own telescope, radio, rocket, and a myriad of other marvelous projects. Inevitably, sooner or later, I would come across an advertisement promising to increase my memory a hundredfold if I would just send in one dollar. The secret would be all mine, postpaid.

I used to dream about that secret. But I never got around to sending in my dollar. Somehow I felt instinctively that memory could not really be bought.

Yet, in a manner of speaking, that is precisely what I was buying when I purchased all those books and magazines in the first place. We do not normally think of the printed word as such, but it is in fact a form of memory, the recorded memory of our civilization, the thoughts and ideas of others transmitted to us through their published words.

Memory, this type of recorded, archival memory, is what sets man apart from the other animals. It is also what sets the computer apart from other machines. Memory extends the human intellect and the computer's information far beyond what either man or the computer could retain single-handedly. This is external memory.

At the same time, the internal memory capacity of both man and machine limits the amount and type of external memory that they can utilize. A computer's internal memory defines its processing capabilities and its software holding capacity.

38

It's as if with a small brain your computer could read only small books.

Essentially, personal computers utilize two types of internal memory. The most basic is the machine memory in which are stored the permanent instructions the computer needs in order to operate. This is the read-only memory called ROM. The instructions stored here are fixed and cannot be changed by the user. The information in ROM remains in the computer even when the power has been shut off. Hence the choice of name for my magazine, though some pleasant wags wrote in, after perusing the first couple of issues, to suggest that ROM really stood for Read Only Magazine.

You will not be dealing personally with ROM when using your computer. The programs stored in ROM are placed there by the manufacturer to monitor such things as the flow of data from the keyboard to the central processing unit, or CPU, which does the actual computing, and from there to the video screen. Their functions are roughly analogous to those controlling your walking or using your hands to peel an orange, tasks which, once learned, are automatic. You may consciously decide to walk faster or slower, but the essence of your movements will remain the same.

What makes you decide to propel yourself more quickly, for example, a driver running a red light as you are crossing the street, is part of the constantly changing information in the world around you. Like such transient information, the programs and data not stored permanently in the computer are put into a second type of internal memory called RAM, or random-access memory. Here new information can be entered and old information removed, and whatever is stored in RAM vanishes as soon as you turn off the power.

RAM is a crucial consideration when you are buying a computer. For RAM, or rather, how much of it your computer has, determines which software you can use and how fast it will run. It is also one of several reasons why, if possible, you should look at the software on the market that interests you *before* you buy a computer.

Somewhere on the cover or within the first few pages of the manual, every software package will list its hardware requirements, including whether you need one disk drive or two, the type of printer required, if any, and so on. There will also usually be a statement as to the number of Ks, or kilobytes, of memory needed to run the program.

The actual execution of the software—the internal calculations of the computer and the binary arithmetic involved—is an interesting topic in itself, and there are many good books on it for the technically minded. But you don't really need to understand the subject in order to use your computer, any more than you need to know about resistance and the movement of electrons in order to use an electric range. What you do need to know is that you can't cook, say, ten pounds of spaghetti in a quart saucepan. It simply won't fit.

Let me take three popular programs from my shelves, Bank Street Writer, TK! Solver, and Lotus 1-2-3, to illustrate. The word processing program Bank Street Writer won't fit into a computer equipped with less than 48K of RAM. TK! Solver, a problem-solving package for scientific and engineering applications geared to the IBM PC, needs 96K to run. Lotus 1-2-3, an accounting and graphics package also for the IBM PC, requires 128K. What's more, while 128K is the minimum for this program, the software is written in such a fashion that it can profitably utilize any extra memory available for faster manipulation of data.

My Apple has 48K of memory, so the Apple version of Bank Street Writer runs just fine on it. My IBM PC used to have 64K, effectively barring the use of both TK! Solver and Lotus 1-2-3. But all was not lost.

Often it is possible to add more RAM to a machine, as it was in the case of my IBM. The RAM of an IBM PC can be expanded all the way up to 512K, which is what mine has now. Whether or not you can add more RAM is yet another important fact to be ascertained before you buy a computer.

Buying extra memory for a computer is almost as easy as sending in the dollar specified in that old *The Boy Mechanic* advertisement, although, unfortunately, this computer memory will cost a lot more. But in order for you to be able to increase the memory capacity of your machine, your computer must have expansion slots. These expansion slots accept "cards," such as the 8K memory board I built.

Add-on memory always comes in multiples of 2K, the most common increments being 16, 32, 64, and 128. The larger memory add-ons predominate today. There are inherent technical limits, however, to the amount of memory you can add.

A computer's memory is circumscribed by the type of microprocessor, or central processing unit, it uses. The microprocessor employed in the Apple II series, for example, is what is known as an eight-bit microprocessor. This means that all the program instructions and all the data employed by an Apple II computer take the form of eight-digit, or eight-bit, binary numbers, like, say, 00101110. Again, there is no need for you to become conversant with binary arithmetic in order to make use of its operations, but you do need to know that an eight-bit computer is limited by design constraints to working directly with only 64K of internal memory.

The memory potential of a sixteen-bit computer is a more complex matter. There are no standard limits to it. Different manufacturers of sixteen-bit computer chips, such as IBM with its AT and Tandy with its Model 2000, each do things their own way. However, at the moment, most sixteen-bit computers come with at least 128K of internal memory. Another 128K, for a total of 256K, is common, and add-on boards often bring the total capacity to over 500K, or half a megabyte, of memory.

Numbers and the confusion they so often generate aside, at this juncture in the development of personal computers, it pays to purchase a sixteen-bit model, as opposed to an eight-bit one, if at all possible. Future software of any significance —and by that I mean the software of the very near future— will require at least 128K of memory.

At the time that I was building the Sol, 8K of memory was considered a fair amount for a personal computer, although some manufacturers were already beginning to provide expansion boards enabling one to add another 8K or even 16K of memory to one's machine.

The optimum amount of memory a personal computer should have had become a hotly debated topic by the time I approached computer buff Stan Veit with a request to do a story on it for *ROM*'s second issue.

Stan had opened what was probably the very first computer

store, and certainly the first on the East Coast. I had come upon it at the back of Polk's Hobby Shop, on Fifth Avenue in Manhattan. Past the model railroad equipment, past the airplane kits and wood-carving knives, at the far rear of the store, I had seen a crowd of people gathered around a few display cases containing what had looked like the overflow from an electronics surplus store. Groups of two or three customers had been browsing among the merchandise of each department, but in the computer section, humanity had been so packed that it had taken me half an hour even to get near the corner where Stan had been frantically trying to answer questions. Mine, on how much memory I needed for the Sol, received the hasty response, "You need more than you have." The article proposal, made at a later but only slightly less hectic moment, was my shortcut to a more detailed answer.

"Memory, Memory, How Much Memory?" appeared in the August 1977 issue of *ROM*, and the gist of Stan's detailed elaboration of the memory theme could be summed up in the same terse reply he had given me originally. His summation was, "As the techniques for manufacturing new and larger chips improve, our microcomputers will change from eight-bit to sixteen-bit and then to thirty-two-bit machines. Tomorrow's 'Tabletop 370' may well use a megabyte of memory. Then someone will come out with an expansion module!"

Stan's tomorrow, at the time an indefinite future day barely conceived, is already here. Personal business computers, such as IBM's PC AT and Tandy's 2000, are both sixteen-bit machines, and they can both handle almost a megabyte (that's 1,000K) of memory. For a brief moment, at least, a few personal computers have more memory available than most of us need. The surplus will last, I should guess, for all of a year or two.

The reason why a megabyte of computer memory will not remain a superfluity for long lies in the realm of software. As computers become more powerful and gain more memory, it becomes possible to run more complex programs on them. Designing software could be described, not incorrectly, as taking advantage of the possible. A program written to work satisfactorily with 48K of memory could be given added features, and thus be made both easier to use and generally more elegant, if it had 128K in which to romp around. So software grows, a new souped-up version for a new souped-up machine somehow almost invariably using the maximum amount of memory available.

The Sol's 8K memory board, diminutive by today's standards, presented no such problems of rudimentariness, for the simple reason that no software to speak of was available at the time when I was soldering it together. Not only did one have to build one's own computer, but once it was assembled, chances were one had to write the programs for it as well.

To see what one was doing with this homemade software, one needed a television set. The window into the computer provided by the television screen prevented potentially disastrous keyboard errors from being swallowed by the machine without one's knowing it. However, one couldn't simply plug a television set into the computer. Today, most computers come equipped with a matching monitor. But in the early history of personal computing, one had to have the right connection before the machine would sing, "I/O, I/O, it's off to work we go."

4: Dial I/O for Machine; or, Getting In and Out of Your Computer

Very early in your peregrinations through the world of personal computing, you will encounter the shorthand signpost I/O. Indeed, it is apt to appear on your screen soon after you turn on your computer for the first time.

There's nothing quite like the message "I/O Error . . ." to make the new user of a computer feel immediately and more than vaguely uncomfortable with computing, as if he or she has inadvertently failed to complete some dread initiation rite. I can conceive of no logical reason why this all too frequently displayed error message could not be made a little more "user friendly," not to mention explanatory.

Then again, I can conceive of no logical reason why, the first time I came across the cryptic I/O in my reading, I immediately thought of portholes. I'm sure that Freud could have made a great deal of my seaborne image. (Actually, I'd prefer to have had Jung exploring my images.) Whatever the case, electronically, portholes almost make sense. In point of fact, I/O is more specifically referred to as the I/O port, or the input/output port.

If you envision your computer as a ship full of electrons, you will notice a lot of them waving out the portholes as if they were about to set forth on a cruise. You wave back, and you're communicating—which is exactly what the I/O is for.

The computer itself, the central processing unit, or CPU, is what does the actual work of computing, in conjunction with the onboard memory. But to do the job, the CPU must be able to communicate with the outside world. It does so through the I/O, the physical connector that allows for the flow of electronic messages to and from such attachments as a printer or other peripheral device.

Consider the keyboard again for a moment. Strictly speaking, the keyboard is not part of the computer itself, even though it may be physically combined with the unit containing the CPU into a single module, as in the case of the Commodore 64. To an engineer, the keyboard remains a peripheral, an attachment connected to, or interfaced with, the CPU by way of the I/O. Video monitors and controls such as joysticks, and those effervescent mice overrunning so many computer desks lately, are likewise peripherals.

Not only does the CPU communicate with the outside world through the I/O, but external components communicate with the CPU by that means as well, often without any human mediation. For example, temperature and pressure sensors can send their monitoring messages directly to the CPU, which can respond by sending out, in turn, messages controlling switches for lights and motors.

All of this electronic communication within a computer system takes place in the binary language of ones and zeros, and it occurs in very precise word lengths. Imagine a language in which every word is composed of eight letters, and you have the language of an eight-bit machine. A machine using sixteen letters to a word is a sixteen-bit machine, and so on.

Whenever data is communicated through the I/O of a digital computer, it is transmitted either serially, that is, one letter

45

at a time, or in parallel fashion, one word at a time. Envision rats deserting the probably sinking ship of my fast-becoming-strained analogy. If eight rats jump out of a porthole one at a time, their message of impending doom is serial. If eight rats abreast jump out at once, it's parallel. The ship may not be sinking any faster in the latter case, but you certainly get the message more quickly.

Parallel transmission is fast. It is also expensive, compared with serial transmission, because the technology is more complex. In addition, it is sometimes difficult to use over long distances, due to the likelihood of electrical interference.

And what, you may well be asking by now, has all this to do with you and your personal computer? Quite a lot, actually. How involved with the technicalities you wish to become depends on your own curiosity, but even as basic a matter as selecting your peripherals requires a modest knowledge of such things as electronic compatibility. Without compatibility, the electronic impulses of your computer won't be able to get out the I/O door and into the world of printers and monitors where you can see the end results of its labors.

For example, a printer like the Smith-Corona TP-1 comes in either a parallel or a serial version. If you buy the parallel version and your computer has a serial printer interface, you will also need to buy a new, matching parallel circuit board, or interface, to match that of the printer.

Knowing that you need a serial port for a serial peripheral does not in itself guarantee a match between your computer and a particular peripheral, however. Even if the plugs on one brand of computers and the sockets on another brand of peripherals actually go together, connecting them may still lead to nothing but smoke and frustration because electronically the units are not compatible. There are a number of design standards governing the construction of electronic components, IEEE-488 for parallel data and RS-232 for serial data being as close to universal as anything is in the not-yet-standardized computer industry.

The bottom line here is that buying a personal computer system is not really like purchasing a component stereo, although that image is often employed. For while just about any turntable will plug into any amplifier, plugging an Apple Imagewriter printer into a Commodore 64 computer will get you nowhere. The best way to determine the true compatibility of computer components is to spend a little time visiting computer stores, asking questions.

In your search, you can pursue one of two courses, either system or component. You can look at complete systems from single manufacturers. In other words, you might consider buying, say, the basic Apple IIe computer, one or two Apple disk drives, an Apple printer, Apple video monitor, and so on.

Using the component approach, you might still buy the basic Apple IIe, but with disk drives from one of the Rana Systems series, which are Apple plug compatible. The Ranas offer more disk memory capacity than the Apple drives do, along with better-designed measures to prevent you from inadvertently overwriting something on a disk that you intended to keep.

Nowhere does the component approach to assembling your personal computer center offer more choice than in the selection of a printer. The printed word conveys information and evokes a mood not only by the content of its expression, but, more subtly, by the very typeface employed as well.

Most readers of mysteries will, upon reading the first line, immediately recognize a book imported from England, as opposed to one printed in the United States. There will be something very British about the type, the use of white space, even the inking involved. These elements in turn will make the mystery more evocative of things both manorial and fish and chippy.

Or take the logo of *The New York Times*. Were it suddenly to appear on the front page of that newspaper set in a modern sans-serif Helvetica rather than in its traditional font, a lot of readers would be startled. A lot would even feel, for a while at least, that the paper wasn't really the *Times* anymore.

The appearance of the printed word may not be crucial. But it does make a difference, however subtle a one, and that is a factor not to be belittled when choosing a printer for a personal computer. Psychologically, the slightly malformed characters produced by dot matrix printers evoke the essence of computerization. With that evocation often comes a sense of hardness, of emotionless technology. Many people react negatively, at once, to an obviously computer-generated missive —in all probability justifiably so.

Whether a computer letter that does not look as if it has been computer generated constitutes a moral fraud is another question. Certainly it does so to at least a minor extent. But the immediate question confronting the would-be buyer is, if you are going to use your computer primarily for printed text (as opposed to pictures, for which you must use a dot matrix printer), do you want the content to start off with a strike against it?

Tastes change, of course. I remember being positively depressed when *The New Yorker,* last of the magazines to use high-quality letterpress printing, switched to offset. The magazine seemed to lose some of its visual crispness. Within a few issues of the change, however, the old, extra-special quality had become but a hazy memory, and one perhaps not very accurate at that. Dot matrix printing may eventually work its artful persuasion on the skeptical in the same way.

Nevertheless, for the next several years, high-class text will remain in the domain of letter-quality printers. Originally very expensive peripherals indeed, these printers are becoming more affordable, on the relative scale of computer equipment, as the demand for reasonably low-cost alternatives increases.

The daisywheel, a simple circular disk with numerous fingers extending from it like narrow flower petals, each bearing a single character, is one type of print head used in the letter-quality printers. The central hub of the removable daisywheel slips onto a drive shaft that rotates the wheel to the selected letter, and a print hammer drives the chosen character in turn onto a ribbon, impressing it on the paper. Another, similar print head is the so-called thimble, which, if you wanted to maintain the flower image, could also be called a tulip. A third is the familiar ball devised by IBM for its Selectric typewriter. All three printing heads offer the advantage of easily interchanged typefaces, although the daisywheel and tulip models are normally faster—an obvious advantage

48

when it's the computer, rather than a mere hunt-and-peck artisan, that's doing the typing.

When you are talking in terms of twelve, twenty, or forty-five characters per second, you can readily see that some pretty fancy fingerwork and precision are involved in the mechanical functioning of letter-quality printers. It's the mechanics concomitant to such speeds, and not the electronics, that you are paying for. A twenty-characters-per-second letter-quality printer costs roughly twice as much as one that plods along at twelve characters per second; a forty-characters-per-second model, three times as much. There are other features that add to the price differential, but as a rule of thumb, you can go by speed costs.

Still speaking of costs, when you are looking at letter-quality printers, make sure you check the price of replacement print elements as well as the price of the machine itself. For one thing, the print elements do eventually wear out. When that happens, you lose the quality you sought in the first place. For another thing, in order to take full advantage of the flexibility in font styles afforded by removable-head printers, you will probably want to assemble a small collection of elements.

A larger, and more continual, expense to be considered is that of ribbon cartridges. These accessories fall into the old "Sell cheap razors and make your money on the blades" category. There's no getting around it either, since a printer without ribbons is really unsuitable for use as anything but a flower press.

Besides print quality, cost, and speed, a fourth consideration in the choice of a printer is convenience of operation. Many factors affect convenience, but in printing, particularly with a letter-quality printer, with which you might want to use high-quality rag bond paper, one of the major hurdles is paper feed.

There are, basically, two types of paper feed. One is the friction variety, which works along the lines of a typewriter roller. The other is pin feed, in which rotating pins pull continuous lengths of paper through the printer. A variation on pin feed often called tractor feed employs pins as well, but in

this case the pin positions are adjustable, so as to accommodate various paper widths. Make sure the printer you choose
can accept the kind of paper you intend to use. If you have
any doubts in the matter, take some samples with you and
either have the salesman demonstrate how the printer works
with your paper or compare your paper with what he has
available, to be sure that you can purchase similar paper in a
form the printer in question will accept.

Both friction and pin feeds use what is called fanfold paper,
a continuous strip perforated at the page breaks. Perforations
are also used, in the case of the pin feed paper, along the
outer edges of the paper, so that the hole-punched strips can
be removed. Once the printer has spewed forth its typed copy
and you have torn all those perforations, you have a sheaf of
not particularly classy-looking typing paper with rather rough
notches.

The art of perforation-making is improving. The pimples
are not quite as noticeable as they used to be. Nevertheless,
if you decide to go to the expense of purchasing a letter-
quality printer, as opposed to a dot-matrix model, you will
probably want to use sheets of regular, rag bond typing paper.

This, however, will require another purchase in addition to
the acquisition of the printer, unless you wish to stand around
and feed the panting platen yourself, one sheet at a time. For
finished results on bond paper, you will need an automatic
sheet feeder.

Because you are again looking at a mechanical product, you
may find that the sheet feeder is as expensive as the printer
itself. But prices are declining, and a letter-quality printer
plus sheet feeder can now be had, from companies like Pri-
mages, for less than a comparable printer alone would have
cost only a couple of years ago.

Make certain that you load and run your prospective printer
several times before you buy it. Loading and paper feed are
two of the weakest links in printing output. Jamming is a
particularly notorious fault of automatic feeders. Even if you
are going to hand-feed your printer single sheets of paper,
you want to be very sure that it can be done easily and
quickly.

50

You will also want to check the number of columns, or characters per line, the printer is capable of producing. For most personal applications, eighty columns is all you need, and that much is provided by most printers. But if you are involved with the financial side of business, you should probably be looking at a 132-column printer, capable of handling spreadsheets and other accounting applications. Of course, you could always use Scotch tape.

Compared to the old clickety-clack of a typewriter, word processing is silence itself—until you turn on the printer. Then you might as well be sitting in a machine gun nest. Printers are a class of machines so noisy that numerous manufacturers have profited by building acoustic cabinets to enclose them and dampen their din. The letter-quality ones are the worst offenders, but dot matrix machines do not escape the criticism.

A more elegant solution than to cover them up would have been to design a quiet printer. But since printers are essentially high-speed mechanical devices, and since hard moving parts do invariably make noise when they are interacting, not much progress has been evident in this direction. Now, however, two distinct and totally different approaches to printing are beginning to make their mark in the world of personal computing. These two approaches are embodied in the new laser and ink jet printers, both of which are not only relatively quiet, but capable of producing near letter-quality text as well as graphics.

Laser printers, which carry an aura straight from science fiction, are still too pricey for most users. The present output quality of the inexpensive ink jet printers, on the other hand, appears for the most part to be just the thing for individuals desirous of obtaining carbons without bothering with originals.

So when the Hewlett-Packard ThinkJet printer arrived for my perusal, I put it on my backup desk and let it sit. After all, the thing was about the size of a dictionary, weighed all of six-and-a-half pounds, and apparently ran off a built-in battery, for heaven's sake.

True, the battery was rechargeable, and the machine could

run using a normal power outlet instead of its battery pack. Still, it had to be a toy. One needed only to look at its price tag to see that. At under $500, it was cheap for a printer—and if there's one thing Hewlett-Packard has always stood for besides well-engineered, quality products, it's comparatively expensive ones.

Nevertheless, things don't sit buried forever, even on my extra, backup desk. So one day I hauled the ThinkJet out from beneath the piles of other yet-to-be-looked-at equipment and plugged it into the Hewlett-Packard 110 portable computer.

The ThinkJet does not have to be used with a Hewlett-Packard computer. There are clones of the printer designed to function with the Apple II computers and the IBM PC. That was another innovation that left me scratching my head, since Hewlett-Packard normally limits itself to HP compatibility.

After connecting the printer to the computer with two idiot-proof cables, I turned to loading the paper. It was then that I noticed the printer had no platen knobs. The feeling that I was dealing with a toy returned. Surprisingly, however, inserting either single sheets or fanfold paper presented no difficulties, and neither type of paper jammed. I began to sense a challenge.

As I was ripping out a page of fanfold after sampling several different qualities of paper—the ThinkJet really works best with the special, high-porosity paper Hewlett-Packard supplies—a small piece of the tractor feed track edging the paper did jam in the rollers. Since it was inaccessible, I left it there and inserted fresh paper. The errant strip popped right out as I did so, and the new paper slid smoothly into place.

Suddenly determined to get a real paper jam, I removed the paper separator, a curved piece of plastic not attached to the machine but carried independently and slipped into two little holding slots when the printer is about to be used. It seemed designed to become lost, and I was curious to see what problems would arise when that presumed inevitability occurred.

Nothing unusual ensued at all. The printer just kept humming along. Actually, "whining" probably better describes its tonal quality. Although it is very quiet by printer standards, the machine is not totally silent.

Even paper so crumpled that normally it would no longer be usable did not jam the rollers. In fact, they smoothed it, at least to some extent, and kept right on cranking out my breathless prose—without any smears, broken type, or degeneration of the print quality to mar the final results.

Determination did win out in the end. I finally managed to jam the printer by taking the rather less than cricket approach of inserting a single piece of paper so askew that it simply would not fit. Overall, however, shenanigans aside, the operation of the HP ink jet printer is remarkably foolproof.

Even replacing the ink cartridge, which needs to be done every five hundred pages or so, is a surprisingly tidy procedure. Instead of having to refill an ink well or insert a new ribbon, you simply replace the whole print head, which costs no more than a ribbon cartridge for the average printer.

To describe the ThinkJet's printing mechanism simply, without going into the technical details, the front of the ink reservoir contains the actual electronics controlling the temperature and flow of ink as it is sprayed onto the paper. There is one unaccustomed step to be remembered in changing print heads. In addition to switching the cartridges, one must also replace a small ink absorber measuring one-quarter by three-quarters of an inch, located to the left of the bail arm. This device is simply a sliver of high-tech blotting paper put there to soak up the squirt of ink that spurts out as the printer is turned on.

The actual printing process is very fast indeed. A truly bidirectional printer depositing type both as the print head travels from left to right, in the ordinary way, and on its return trip right to left, the ThinkJet spews out copy at a rate of 150 characters per second.

While the HP printer limits you to one font style, you do have a selection of four pitches, or sizes, along with boldface, underlining, and overstrike options. Another option is graphics, using a matrix format of ninety-six by ninety-six dots per inch.

Squeezing 9,216 dots into an inch produces very sharp

53

print for pictures and graphs as well as type fonts. There is still a considerable distance to be covered in design work before ink jet printers can match letter-quality ones, but it looks as if they should overtake the dot matrix printers in quality very soon.

A printer is but one means by which the I/O mechanism delivers the computer's contents to the outside world. Another way is through the monitor. But whereas printers come in a great diversity of forms, monitors have about them a certain deceptive sameness.

The monitor is the only component of a computer system to come close to being standardized. It also seems to be the one aspect of computing to generate no fears or phobias in even the most rank neophyte. To a generation nurtured by television, after all, electronic images are as familiar as the breakfast cereal so often consumed in front of them. Thus it comes as a surprise to many people that a video display, that now ubiquitous picture window into the computer, is a relatively new addition to the machine.

Before personal computers appeared on the scene, no continuous visual display enlivened the technology of electronic data processing. Programmers did their thing on paper, believe it or not. When everything was in order, the code laboriously arrived at was keyed into the computer. The program ran unseen by human eyes.

The same held true for the data used with the program. It was entered and processed undramatized. Only the final results were made evident, in printed copy.

The use of a monitor with the modern personal computer does not make us privy to all the internal workings of the machine. But it has accustomed us to being able to watch at least a semblance of what is going on throughout our endeavors at the console.

Perhaps it is this taking of the display for granted, perhaps it is the fact that when buying a computer most people do not yet think in component terms as they would in purchasing a stereo, perhaps it is simply a matter of the easy way out—but when it comes to acquiring a computer monitor, most people do very little looking around. This can be a mistake.

One has more contact with the monitor than with any other single element of a computer system, including the keyboard. So, for comfort's sake if for no other, a good monitor is essential to good computing. Even computers, such as the Compaq and the Kaypro, that come with their own diminutive, built-in monitors are candidates for a supplementary screen.

The question is, what constitutes a good monitor? The answer, for the most part, comes in pixels.

Pixel is short for *picture element,* the smallest unit that can be turned on or off on the display screen. In a black and white display, each pixel requires one bit of memory, one on/off signal, black or white. The more—and thus the smaller—pixels a screen is capable of displaying, the sharper the resulting picture will be.

From the eye's point of view, the visual process of looking at an image portrayed on a monitor screen is similar to looking at a photograph. The representation produced by a monitor with large pixels is somewhat akin to a grainy photograph, while that of a monitor with a greater number of small pixels more resembles a fine-grained picture. The small-pixel video screen image and the fine-grained photograph both appear sharper and clearer.

The comparison is apt in another way, for where pixel power really counts is in graphics, in computer pictures. It is somewhat less crucial in applications like word processing, where the mind assists the eye in translating symbols, however fuzzy, into meaningful representations, and where aesthetics is not a strident issue. This is in no way to imply that the eye does not appreciate clarity in the verbal arts, of course.

Alphanumeric characters on the screen are produced in the computer by a character-generating ROM. They are fixed, and in any case they need not be as sharply defined as pictures. People do accept slingshot-shaped *Y*'s and square *O*'s. They are less able to identify with square faces, even in cartoons. So if you are interested in computer graphics, you will probably want the most pixels you can get.

Like everything else, pixels are not free, which is why a number of personal computers use a standard television set

55

for their display. A good color monitor costs $500 or $600, a color television set less than half of that.

But the maximum resolution of a television receiver is 256 by 192 pixels, that is, 256 dots horizontally and 192 dots vertically, for a total of 49,152 pixels, give or take a couple around the edges of the screen. By comparison, the IBM PC in its high-resolution mode has a display of 640 by 200 pixels, for a total of 128,000. The Epson KX-30, so far available only in Japan, has a 1,024 by 640 display, which brings the pointillism up to a staggering 655,360 pixels per picture.

Even in the case of a monochrome unit, color is a consideration. Currently, white on black is deemed the least desirable, a green or amber background with darker letters of the same color being the hue of choice. Amber is presently a hot concept. But not everyone finds it more restful than green. The qualities that really count on screen are resolution, contrast, and the absence of flicker, though not necessarily in that order.

I am personally very adversely affected by flicker. Thus I rate it as the most important of the three factors except where graphics is concerned. Others are willing to overlook a certain amount of flicker if it means having greater sharpness. The final test for any screen, be it green, amber, or full color, is whether your eyes are comfortable with it over a long period of time.

There are two distinct kinds of color monitors, composite and RGB (red, green, blue). Here the difference is more clear-cut than the variations among monochrome types, and it is defined by the technology involved. Monitors using the RGB format always produce a sharper image, because each of the three colors is brought to the display as an independent signal. Composite color utilizes a single, compound signal. It's like pumping a rainbow into your set. Inside the cathode ray tube of the display, the rainbow is split by means of three electron-beam guns into the colors needed for the picture.

While the resolution of an RGB color monitor is sharper than that of one utilizing composite color, it is not as sharp as that of a monochrome unit. Because of this, some people end

56

up buying two monitors, a monochrome for such tasks as word processing and a color monitor for graphics endeavors.

This double expenditure might seem excessive at first glance. But the fact is that using a color monitor for a lot of word processing almost inevitably leads to eyestrain, whereas a monochrome monitor naturally cannot display the color graphics used in charting or, for that matter, in games and other entertainment programs.

Whichever type of display you decide will meet the majority of your personal computing needs, the only way to choose among the various models on the market is through a side-by-side comparison of your leading contenders. Have the dealer run a couple of programs containing both text and graphics so that you can view them on the several screens, preferably simultaneously. Compare the results.

First, check the sharpness of the text characters. Pay particular attention to those appearing at the edges of the screen. There can be quite a difference between the centerstage image and its peripheries. Look closely for flickers and wavers, especially when text is being scrolled and when the screen is being changed.

Next, compare the degree of jaggedness in the curved lines and circles of the graphics displays. Also watch for color bleeds or shadows. Vary the contrast, tint, and color so that you can see what range of adjustment is possible. Then step back and look at the pictures from various angles to check how much glare the screens produce under different light conditions.

Finally, once your eyes have given the go-ahead, but before you plunk down the cash, remember to match the monitor to the computer. Buying a top-of-the-line display for an inexpensive computer won't get you the great picture you were expecting. A low-end computer simply cannot produce the high-quality signal a first-class monitor needs in order to give its all.

• • •

If the various components of a computer system are so perversely individual and potentially at odds in their design, what is to tie them all together into a working unit? Physically, and assuming that they are at least theoretically compatible, they are connected by means of cables. Electronically, they are melded by that remarkable software, invisible to you and me, known as the computer's operating system. One of the great internal mysteries of the computer, this is a phenomenon having no equivalent in our day-to-day mechanical world.

If you plug in a toaster, drop some bread into the slot, and push down the lever, in a short while you will be rewarded with toast. If you want a second slice a little darker or a little lighter than the first, you can turn a timer dial to the appropriate setting. The sequence of tasks leading to your goal is easy and straightforward.

If you are making a complete breakfast, matters become a bit more complicated. To begin with, there's the question of the bacon. Assuming you like your eggs fried in bacon fat, you have to start the rashers first. Then, when they are partially crisped, you slide some eggs onto the griddle. As they are sizzling away, you suddenly realize you need orange juice. But meanwhile the toast is going to be done too soon to stay hot. So you pop it up early by hand, open the freezer door in search of some orange juice concentrate and. . . .

Now you are functioning as an operating system for the Great American Breakfast Machine. You have become the interface between the hardware (coffeepot, griddle, toaster) and the software (the strategy for producing a successful breakfast with all the dishes ready at the same time).

Make an imaginary and rather crude substitution of a printer for your coffeepot, a video display monitor for the toaster, a keyboard for the griddle, and so on. Substitute, finally, an operating system for yourself, and you have an up-and-running computer system. Without an operating system, at best there would be chaos in the computer. More likely, nothing would get done at all.

But not all computer systems perform tasks in the same way, just as not everyone cooks in the same way. Apple computers, for example, use an operating system called Apple

DOS or, more recently, ProDOS. It is quite different from the IBM PC-DOS and from the TRS-80 DOS used by Radio Shack computers. If you want to use some software that requires Apple DOS and your machine happens to run IBM PC-DOS, you're plumb out of luck, because the different operating systems used by the different personal computers are incompatible. You can't make coffee in a toaster.

The incompatibility of the various operating systems arose in the first place because, like temperamental cooks, the computer manufacturers all wanted to do things their own way. Nevertheless, there did evolve a few operating systems that were adopted in common by a limited number of different brands of computers. The use of the same operating system, as, for instance, in Compaq's cloning of IBM DOS, allows for a transportability of software. That is, a program that runs on one brand of computer will also run on another utilizing the same operating system.

To people accustomed to the idea that if you have a cassette player or a phonograph, you can go out and buy any tape cassette or record and expect it to play on your machine, this may not sound like exactly a revolutionary step forward. But for the computer industry, such standardization would be. Chances are that in the future most personal computers will use one of a limited number of standardized operating systems. Meanwhile, however, fragmentation reigns in DOS country.

Early in the history of personal computers, a particular operating system called CP/M, or Control Program for Microcomputers, became a dominant force, outdistancing a number of lesser-used systems. Now MS-DOS, the disk operating system marketed by Microsoft Corporation and adopted by IBM, is taking the driver's seat in one version or another in most new personal computers. The vast majority of the software being written for microcomputers today utilizes one or the other of these two operating systems. So let's take a closer look at them.

CP/M, the granddaddy of personal computer operating systems, was developed in 1973 by Gary Kildall of Digital Research Corporation. At the time, personal computers existed only as experimental prototypes constructed by a few innovative hobbyists.

Because, as we have noted, computer software inevitably has bugs, or errors, in need of eradication, and because it is almost always in need of updating to accommodate new developments, the original CP/M version, V1.0, was eventually replaced by V1.3, then V1.4, V2.0, and so on. The latest modification, as of this writing, is V3.0.

One of the changes in CP/M V3.0 is an increase in the speed with which a computer using this operating system can handle its diverse tasks. Another is an expanded capacity to control more memory on a floppy disk. Controlling the floppy disks is one of the most important functions of an operating system for personal computers, which is why, in fact, many companies refer to it as the disk operating system, or DOS, even though it performs many other duties.

CP/M has four main parts: BDOS, the Basic Disk Operating System; CCP, or Console Command Processor; BIOS, the Basic Input/Output System; and TPA, or Transient Program Area. Each of these components controls a specific set of operations.

BDOS, the Basic Disk Operating System, manages the floppy disk drives. It tells the computer when to activate a drive, when to read information from the disk, and when to write information onto it. More importantly, it tells the computer where on the disk information is to be found or stored. In the process of formatting, as we have seen, DOS maps out on the disk the appropriate series of memory locations and builds a directory to help in locating them. On a clear disk your computer could search forever.

BDOS could be regarded as the rough equivalent of an automatic filing clerk for, say, recipe cards. An uninitialized disk is like the recipe file itself, filled with blank cards. Once formatted, it's a file with alphabet dividers in place. A recipe for Leek Soup can now be filed under L, Sachertorte under S, and so on.

Before you can put any information onto a floppy disk, you have to get it into the computer by way of the keyboard, touch pad, or other entry device. Here, too, the operating system plays a crucial role. The second component of CP/M, the CCP, or Console Command Processor, is what takes the character whose key you strike on the keyboard, say the letter x, and translates it into something the computer can swallow.

BIOS, the Basic Input/Output System, directs the flow of information back and forth between the computer itself and the disk drive, video monitor, printer, telephone modem, or whatever other conceivable peripheral might currently be hooked up to it.

Likewise, the actual applications software you are running, say an accounting or a word processing program, is stored and monitored by the computer in the TPA, the Transient Program Area.

IBM PC-DOS, developed by Microsoft for IBM's personal computers, is basically a modified version of Microsoft's own MS-DOS. These two operating systems call for different commands to cue the computer, but they control essentially the same maneuvers as CP/M does, and in fact they use many of the same commands. The biggest distinction to be made between them from the user's point of view, frankly, is that, with the IBM imprimatur behind it, MS-DOS in its various forms can probably be expected to become as much of an industry standard as anything is in personal computing, barring the not unlikely eventuality that IBM decides to develop its own operating system.

Need one really know all about these goings-on within an operating system? Well, yes and no.

Sometimes it's enough to know that if you have an IBM computer using PC-DOS as its operating system, you won't be able to run any of the numerous software packages written for CP/M, and vice versa—unless your computer can be modified to accept a second operating system. Some manufacturers are now adding special boards enabling their computers to run two different operating systems as needed. Reminiscent of those kitchen scales displaying their measurements in both the metric and the avoirdupois systems, these hybrids are not necessarily an elegant solution, but they do bridge a period of transition.

There are instances in which a basic understanding of at

least the elementary operating system commands is essential to the efficient operation of your computer. For example, in the case of both CP/M and PC-DOS, typing DIR will cause the computer to list all the information files on the disk in its drive, an invaluable aid when you are unable to recall what is on a disk that you have not used for a long time.

Again, you might have tucked your grandmother's old recipe for raisin bread away on disk somewhere, but if you don't happen to remember the exact name under which you filed it —and due to the idiosyncrasies of computerized filing, one is almost invariably obliged to abbreviate file names to the point where they become virtually unrecognizable—you could spend a lifetime staring at the disk, unable to extract the recipe from the computer. By simply typing DIR, on the other hand, you can call up the disk's "table of contents," wherein you will find a file labeled GRBRD that you recognize as being the wanted item. You might even discover another wonderful recipe you had filed away as well and forgotten all about.

Having found the recipe for Grandma's raisin bread again, you might also find that you want to forget about it forever. By entering ERASE, in the case of IBM PC-DOS, or ERA, in the case of CP/M, you can eliminate the file. It's not like crumpling up a recipe card and throwing it away, however. You erase only a small part of the disk, and the space vacated can be filled with new information.

The COPY command in PC-DOS is what you use to create a file for the first time. It is also, as the word implies, what you use to copy information from one disk onto another, or, for that matter, onto the same disk under a new name. CP/M uses the COPY command followed by the letter C to copy a diskette and COPY followed by an F in formatting a disk.

An intimate knowledge of a computer's operating system is something only a dedicated programmer will acquire. But anyone who uses a computer at all will need to become acquainted with the basic half-a-dozen or so crucial DOS commands. One nearly painless way to acquire such a working knowledge is through an interactive tutorial program like Professor DOS, from Individual Software, created for users of the

IBM PC and compatible computers. DOS tutorial graduates are rarely fazed by either operating systems or the more complex software packages requiring one to put DOS on their disks before using them.

Consider the popular integrated software package Lotus 1-2-3, which combines interactive spreadsheet, graphics, and information management programs. Without knowing how to transfer DOS from your DOS disk to the right spot on the Lotus disk, you cannot run this software. The simple DOS command INSTALL is what effects the transfer. All you have to do is speak a little DOS.

That's the situation today, for which we can be thankful. But it was not always thus. By the time I had my Sol assembled, operating system in place and ready to run, Processor Technology had vanished from the face of Silicon Valley. So, for that matter, had most of the other early personal computer manufacturers, among them MITS, IMSAI, PolyMorphic Systems, Midwest Scientific, Seals Electronics, Technical Design Labs, and the Digital Group.

Like so many personal computer owners in those days, I was left with an orphan, a machine for which I could no longer get parts or help. More to the point, I had a machine with an extinct operating system for which no one would ever write any software. In other words, my machine could do nothing, unless I laboriously programmed it myself.

I was also stuck with a magazine the vast majority of whose advertisers no longer existed. That made collecting on the accounts receivable for their ads somewhat difficult.

The smart-money people in publishing, from those at *The New York Times*, Ziff-Davis, McGraw-Hill, and Warner Communications to venture capitalist Alan Patricof, who originally arranged the funding of the hugely successful *New York* magazine, assured me without reservation that there was absolutely no future in personal computing. Certainly no publisher with a head on his shoulders was about to put up any money for a periodical devoted to such a minor field. I couldn't even give *ROM* away. In the end, I turned its subscription list over to *Creative Computing*, so that the faithful *ROM* subscribers would at least receive something by way of a computer magazine for their money, and wrote the venture off as a very expensive M.B.A. acquired in the manner of a real-life Harvard case approach.

Then I went back to writing full time, with an occasional foray into the relaxing world of fishing down on our pond, where I could at least eat heartily from my efforts. The Sol had enough heft to be used as an anchor for the canoe, but the shape was a bit bulky for that purpose, so the machine was relegated to a back shelf in the more remote reaches of my study closet.

Every now and then some news about personal computing would come trickling up to the farm. I paid it no heed. The house had a second and a third mortgage on it now, courtesy of *ROM*. The children had saved up their money and bought horses, and somehow they had smooth-talked Susan and myself into each getting one as well. Commerce had introduced ultrapasteurized cream into our environs, upsetting me to the point where I had gone out and purchased a Jersey of mellow disposition so that we could have real cream again. All in all, things were quite busy enough without any computers around to fuss over.

For some four years our life remained reasonably pastoral —until the middle of 1982, when, out of the blue, Rick Flaste, editor of *The New York Times* Tuesday Science Times section, called. How were my computers, he wanted to know.

"Nonexistent," I replied, only a little regret mixed with my relief. Neither feeling was to remain intact for long. A week later I was winging it towards Houston and the National Computer Conference on assignment from the *Times*.

Personal computing had come a long way, I was told. It was now a mature and prospering multimillion-dollar industry. Respect was written all over it in corporate marquee lights. Surely now I would be able to unearth the answer to that question, "What do I do with a personal computer?"

5: Five Years Later and Still Playing Games

My Houston-bound flight for the 1982 National Computer Conference, or NCC, was packed with computer consorts of every description, from newly made millionaires to those who would not, even in their dreams, confront the IRS for at least another six months. We were all locked together in that tubular equalizer of modern aviation technology where the $400 difference between first class and the rest of the world was a two-inch extra seat allowance and real fake silverware instead of fake fake silverware.

With my elbows neatly tucked beneath my shoulders, yet still unable to avoid rubbing those of a portly gentleman overflowing his seat on my right, and a porthole once permeable to vision but now permanently fogged over on my left, I attempted to read a newspaper folded subway fashion to expose a quarter of its surface at a time. A story devoted to the latest in Polish jewelry, a tiny electronic component, the resistor, caught my eye. The diminutive device, worn as a pin, had been requisitioned from the realm of high technology by Solidarity members for service as a badge of protest against martial law.

The adoption by the masses of such an abstruse symbol struck me as an act of more than political significance. In a very real, if minute, manner, it heralded the end of the mechanical age.

On a much grander scale, and infused with more distracting bread and circuses than the most repressive political regime could hope to muster, this very same announcement was to be made thematically at the NCC. The mechanical age was manifestly crumbling.

Only four years earlier, as *ROM* magazine floated belly up and I abandoned the computer keyboard for a fishing rod, the NCC had consigned small personal computers to the outlying booths and basements of its exhibit halls. There was even talk, at the annual computer cabal to plot the near future of data communications, of excluding these tiny upstarts from future shows entirely. Psychologically, they detracted from the master movers' mystique. A chicken in every pot and a car in every garage were fine economic goals for the world at large, but a computer in every home might weaken the power base of the industry beyond acceptable limits. Besides, personal computing wasn't professional.

Yet at NCC '82 personal computers, or micros, as the trade called them, dominated not only every nook and cranny but center stage as well. After all, what do you do when a tiny upstart with a name like Apple backs out of the family garage and records sales of over a quarter of a billion dollars for the first six months of fiscal 1982? You join forces with it, what else?

Hence IBM was there with a brand-new personal computer. So were Digital Equipment, Data General, Texas Instruments, and other giants, suddenly roused to a feverish production mode. Such Pacific phoenixes from World War II as Sony, Mitsubishi, and Panasonic brought micros, and in the far reaches of the most distant exhibit hall, the Taiwanese

66

established a beachhead with their prototype micro. The Occident could rest assured that the electronic East slept no more.

Personal computers were everywhere I turned. As one blister-footed conventioneer was later to remark, his green-glazed eyes reflecting video screens after three days of wandering the mirrored halls of computerland, "There wasn't anything radically new and unexpected. But everything was cheaper, faster, and smaller to an unprecedented degree."

The statement heard perhaps most often among the close to 100,000 people attending the show was "I want one of those." Not "I want one of those for my company," but "*I* want one of those, for myself." That must certainly be the essence of personal computing. So its time, for better or worse, had obviously come. But why?

As I began to reinfiltrate the mysterious world of electronics, I sensed that people, no matter how much they thought they wanted a personal computer, were still puzzled by the question of what to do with one. There had been a change in the machines since the early smoke-and-mirror days when they had first emerged from Silicon Valley. Physically, they had become sleeker, showier products, and some of their hallmark self-deprecating humor had been whisked away by starched-collared managers with M.B.A.'s. Kentucky Fried Computers had been renamed a more somber North Star Computers, and what was probably the all-time unsurpassed descriptive name for a computer company, Thinker Toys, had given way to a more mundane and respectable Morrow.

Software, too, had evolved, if perhaps less exuberantly than the computers themselves. Its trappings had acquired a professional air. Earlier in the game, when a disk made an appearance, it was packaged in a plastic baggie, along with a few sheets of incomprehensible instructions produced by a copier. Now software was being marketed in fancy shrink-wrapped boxes enclosing a disk plus a sheaf of still incomprehensible instructions, quite often running to hundreds of pages, in loose-leaf format so that "updates"—that is, corrections—could readily be inserted by the customer, who was still the guinea pig.

67

The most remarkable thing about the new software, however, was the fact that it was available at all. There were real programs to be had. Not merely a small selection of computer languages, such as BASIC, put on disk for the convenience of do-it-yourself programmers, but a whole range of real, honest-to-goodness applications software to make the computer actually do something, was available. There was software for word processing, for number crunching with spreadsheets, for financial projections, for manipulating stock portfolios, and, of course, for playing games.

Faced with these multifarious software options, most people, given their druthers, seemed to gravitate toward the games. My overwhelming impression of the NCC, in fact, was one of fun and games for all, with exhibitors occasionally playing the millionaire.

Personal computing is not alone in catering to this impulse in our lives. Our everyday existence, after all, is replete with references to such things as war games, role playing, simulation, and projection, and it is becoming more and more difficult to distinguish the evening television news from the preceding sitcom and the following smash-'em-up adventure series.

Some two hundred thousand years ago, man's crude tools began to take on an aesthetic air. To their former pure utilitarianism was added an element of design that could easily have been pronounced useless, but that nonetheless eventually became part and parcel of all his artifacts. If a quality of gamesmanship is now being added to our endeavors as well, it is not for me to proclaim that union morally good or bad. What seems to me indisputable, however, is that electronics, and more particularly computing, has both facilitated and fostered this turn of events.

It was this conclusion, seemingly foregone, upon which I was reflecting as I returned home from that computer gathering in Houston with perhaps a slight case of electronic overexposure and a suitcaseful of software—mostly games. The particularly bumpy landing of my plane at Bradley Field, north of Hartford, Connecticut, jolted me from my reverie, bringing to mind, perhaps by way of comic relief, an incident that had occurred earlier that year.

We'd been about fifteen minutes out of Fort Lauderdale in a friend's Aero Commander, its 750-horsepower engines purring along and the boat-filled Atlantic below looking particularly clear to my New England eyes, when suddenly one of my daughters yelled from the passenger compartment, "Daddy, are you flying this plane?"

Our rather sporadic seesaw course had made the answer obvious. But Wayne Stayton, the pilot, had let me continue exercising, for the very first time, my rather dubious aeronautical talents. Familial flak aside, I enjoyed that flight.

· · ·

Shortly after my return from the NCC, I found myself sitting at the controls of a single-engine Cessna 182 cruising at three thousand feet over Lake Michigan. After crashing on takeoff, I had finally managed to become airborne. Even then, it had been a rather waltzy maneuver, what with the plane taking a shortcut across the runway dividers. Luckily, Meigs Field, the plane's home base, seemed to have grass runways indistinguishable from the rest of the ground save for the white center stripe.

Although I had at last conquered a simple takeoff, and although I had even managed to circle the John Hancock Building—at considerably closer range than would have been approved by the FAA—I was still overcompensating much of the time, flying in the rather wavy fashion of my venture in the Aero Commander. At cruising altitude, however, the plane almost seemed to fly itself, and so, stewardess service not being provided, I decided to make myself a cup of coffee and a Virginia ham sandwich with Fontina cheese on pumpernickel to devour while furthering my education as a pilot. I put the plane on a compass course of 180 degrees south, heading, I hoped, toward the Greater Kankakee Airport. Then, sandwich in hand, I began diligently reading the instruction manual.

Half an hour spent studying the manual, meanwhile making only minor adjustments to the plane's flight pattern in the calm blue sky, left me with an overwhelming impression of problems ahead. As it happened, my worst fears were to be realized. "Correct and safe landing is the most challenging

69

part of flying," the instructions informed me. By the time I
touched ground at Kankakee, "challenging" wasn't a strong
enough word for me.

I simply couldn't get the Kankakee runway lined up properly for a good approach. Finally, I put the plane into a slow
circle above the airport and telephoned Wayne in Florida.
After listening to my account of the situation, he suggested
that I set my radio to 121.5, the International Emergency
Frequency. Unfortunately, my radio wasn't working.

In the end, via an intercom linking the pilot's compartment
to the telephone in the house, Wayne talked me down. At
sixteen hundred feet, I cut the power to half, bringing my
airspeed down to eighty knots, and set the flaps to twenty
degrees. I was supposed to be four miles from the runway on
my glide pattern, but a little miscalculation upset my smooth
descent. As I was trying to bank to the left, I swung around
too sharply, overcompensated to the right, tried to get the
nose up, and finally entered a merry-go-round spin. "Crash,"
the computer display informed me.

All this is not to say that Microsoft's Flight Simulator gives
you a view of the world as it really is through the windshield
of a Cessna 182, or any other plane. The graphics are of the
stick-figure variety, and the green grass is visible right
through the Hancock Building's reddish skeletal structure.
But given the state of the art in personal computers, and especially in graphics, this program, created by Bruce Artwick,
is very good.

It is the more so because it runs in real time. My flailing
about in the blue yonder of the video screen in search of an
airport actually consumed almost forty minutes, which is the
flight time it would have taken a plane to navigate my circu-
itous route in the real skies yonder.

Furthermore, the display panel occupying the lower half of
the video screen has a full complement of functioning instruments in need of constant monitoring. Included are airspeed
and attitude indicators, an altimeter, a directional gyro, a rate-
of-climb indicator, a compass, a clock, a carburetor heat indicator, a magneto switch position indicator, and more. There's
even a NAV, or navigational radio, for tuning in the VOR

(very-high-frequency omnidirectional range) navigational aid.

In the manual there are also navigation maps indicating the VOR frequencies and terminals. It is unfortunate that the manual itself does not have an index, however. One of my few criticisms of the package, this is an inexcusable oversight in a hundred-page volume intended to elucidate a program as complex as Flight Simulator.

And complex it is. Not only are there all those instruments to worry about, but weather, seasonal, and time variables as well. Flying conditions can be made to range from a sunny, summer afternoon to a stormy, winter night. There is even a reliability factor which, when set to less than 100 percent, introduces such unexpected problems as engine failure. The realistic flying environment mode, as distinct from the easy flight conditions mode in which I was struggling along, incorporates everything from iced-up carburetors and improperly functioning altimeters to snow or mud ready to engulf the plane should you go off the runway.

Flight Simulator has become a benchmark in deciding whether a computer is IBM-compatible or not, whether the clone can successfully run software designed for the IBM PC. "If it can run this," the argument goes, "it can run anything."

Part of the attractiveness of Flight Simulator as a test program has to do with its complexity and its heavy reliance on graphics, which is one of the most difficult aspects of a program for a clone to cope with. But, let's face it, a great deal of its popularity has to do with the fact that it's just plain fun. Would you rather haul gravel in a pickup truck for twenty miles or take a Porsche for a spin around Le Mans?

• • •

Another kind of challenge, no less enjoyable, if in a different fashion, is to be found in Rocky's Boots, a software package from The Learning Company. Using the computer's unique, if limited, pedagogical potential, this program is devoted to a task rather appropriately computerized, namely, that of teaching the logical underpinnings of computers themselves.

Someone new to computing is apt to find the fundamental

jargon of the process—terms like *floppy disk*, *ROM*, and *Control C*—enough to induce at least a mild case of computerphobia. Imagine, then, how that same novitiate feels when confronted with the more advanced elements of digital logic, such as and-gates, or-gates, and not-gates, in all their stark schematic configurations. Such things are enough to send almost anyone scurrying off to the beach with a thick, cheap escape novel. Yet once you start running Rocky's Boots, it's pretty hard to turn it off and pick up a book.

The program is sold as a game for seven-year-olds and up, but there is much more to it than there is to the popular shoot-'em-up arcade-type games. In fact, there is more to it than there is to most of the programs being billed as educational software today. An electronic Erector Set of the mind, Rocky's Boots leaves the player surprisingly well versed in the basic concepts of logic.

Remembering my own intimidating, if at the same time fascinating, introduction to logic and Boolean algebra—both subjects, I might add, have long since vanished into the cobwebs of my mind—I was frankly amazed to see my daughters Tanya, then nine years old, and Genevieve, twelve, begin to conceptualize such complex logic sequences as "If A, then B or C, depending on the state of D." I don't mean to imply that Rocky's Boots is a complete, self-contained course in logic. It couldn't be, since the program comes on a single floppy disk. But it does provide an unexpectedly sound foundation in sequential reasoning.

The early sections of the program are rather slow. The first demonstrates how to move a cursor, in this case a large orange one, either by means of the keyboard or with a joystick. The second section is on building machines. It covers the rudiments of connecting wires, sensors, on/off switches, clocks, noise-making clackers, and similar components to produce a functional electronic device. You are shown how to pick up a component with the cursor, connect it to another component, and activate it by running electricity into the socket.

In the more advanced sections of the program, you pick up various spare parts from storerooms and take them into the practice rooms allotted for assembly work. Once the kids discovered the transportability of objects, they dragged spare components, even from the demonstration rooms, along with them wherever they went. Tanya in particular became a veritable pack rat, hauling extra clocks, flip-flops, and delays with her from room to room, "just in case."

"Knives" are used to "cut" connections once they have been made so that the parts can be reassembled in a different fashion. Personally, being of a "right tool for the right job" mentality, at least philosophically, I'd have preferred the program to use wirecutters for the job.

Inappropriate tool aside, the program certainly does lend itself to experimentation. One of Genevieve's early comments, "Let's go to the practice rooms and figure out how to do it without getting instructions," was typical of the response it inspires. So was her reaction on being presented with a demonstration of how oscillators work. "Let's make one of those in real life," she said.

The final, and by far the largest, segment of the program is Rocky's Challenge, a choice of games to play using the machines you have learned how to make. Working out of the half-dozen storage rooms filled with logic gates, timers, clackers, and wires, you assemble everything you think you might need to solve such problems as how to eliminate all the crosses and blue circles from a set of symbols pictured on the screen or all the diamonds preceding a cross in a moving stream of shapes. Once you think you have the solution to a particular problem in hand, you plug in, on screen, Rocky's boots, to "boot out" the pieces chosen by your logic circuit.

The early problems, like eliminating all blue triangles, are easily solved by a young child. Later ones, like getting rid of "diamonds or purple but not both," as the program succinctly put the problem, are more difficult. In fact, Susan and I were up till three o'clock in the morning with that particular one, the solution still eluding us. It's times like that when a columnist appreciates his job. Presenting our problem in print elicited a number of responses offering the correct solution. The replies, I might add, came from professional engineers and research and development people, not children.

A second program from The Learning Company released a

year later, Robot Odyssey I, is even more complex and en-grossing than Rocky's Boots. The player, first pictured on the screen as being fast asleep, falls out of bed and into a deep hole, Alice in Wonderland style, thereby entering Robotrop-olis. The object of the game is to make one's way back to the real world from the maze of sewers, skyways, and subways landscaping this robot-inhabited, underground domain. Ge-nevieve and Tanya had been eagerly awaiting this game ever since they had heard it was to be released as a sequel to Rocky's Boots. Luckily, since Robot Odyssey I is geared to the teenage user, they were a year older by the time it arrived.

"Move on to the eye and activate the robot's periscope. . . ."

"You can even put robots inside of robots. Isn't that neat?"

"Bring that extra energy crystal along. I always bring every-thing with me. . . . Don't drop it there. I want a neat and or-derly robot."

"Can't we pick up two crystals at once?"

"No."

"Bother." (Sometimes I wonder if we spent too much time reading Pooh books to the kids.)

"Hey, look, you can hide an object inside the robot and the sensor doesn't detect it. . . ."

"You need to split it with a nor-gate there."

The conversation between my two daughters, punctuated with the clicks and clacks of the computer keys, would have been unimaginable a mere five years ago between a couple of kids ten and thirteen years old. Yet here were Tanya and Genevieve, the latter a self-proclaimed computer dyslexic, wholly absorbed in the task of designing a robot.

The props of Robot Odyssey I may be those of the standard joystick-controlled computer game, but there all similarity ends. The Learning Company game is an exacting lesson, at the young-adult level, in the logic of electronic microengi-neering, and those who weather extended sessions with this program will probably have a greater comprehension of logic circuits than a college engineering student graduating in the fifties had. In Robot Odyssey I, the player actually designs functional, self-motivated robots, complete with thrusters to move themselves by, bumpers to sense obstacles with, grabbers to pick things up for them, periscopes for vision, and so on.

An on-disk tutorial called Robot Anatomy takes the player step by step through the inner workings of an elementary robot. Two other tutorials, Toolkit and Chip Design, are essential to an understanding of the options available for one's robots.

Toolkit shows you how to build the various complex circuits required to make a robot perform such tasks as finding its way through a maze by itself. These circuits are joined together with a soldering gun, included in the on-screen tool kit along with an assortment of the basic logic circuits, such as flipflops, and-gates and nor-gates, and nodes, needed in one's design work.

Chip Design carries the player's microengineering education one step further. Instead of building circuits in a robot, you design and build actual, if rudimentary, integrated circuit chips, similar to the complex ones found inside a computer, containing whole series of logic commands. These self-contained circuits can then be used to replace a whole batch of normal wiring, just as they can in the real world.

Copies can be made of any prototype chip you design, which saves you tedious repeat operations. It is even possible to build a chip into another chip, which allows you to incorporate time delays and other routines required for developing maze strategies.

These strategies must be thought out rather carefully. The first time Genevieve and Tanya delved into Robotropolis, when they were designing a robot to pick up an energy crystal and move it to another room in one of the mazes, they inadvertently introduced an error in the logic circuit that was to make the robot drop the crystal where they wanted it deposited.

"It won't let go!" was the frustrated human cry.

"This isn't fair. I want a replay." In mock anger, Genevieve picked up the robot with the cursor and smashed it against the maze wall, trying in vain to make it release the crystal, before turning to other, more logical approaches to the problem. The final solution took nearly three hours, although,

75

from what I could determine, it seemed like minutes to the girls.

All of a player's logic circuits and designs can be saved for future use. This is fortunate, since, to judge from the above episode, the running time for the game would seem to be somewhere in the neighborhood of two to six months of steady play. At that rate, Robot Odyssey I could well turn out to be an electronic Dungeons and Design Your Own Dragons.

There are some minor problems besetting the program, for the most part not of its own making. A very small black and white Robotropolitan map of the terrain in which the adventure takes place is provided in the manual. One is supposed to photocopy this map and, by rolling part of it up, turn it into a three-dimensional guide to the maze. It doesn't really work. A large, posterlike diagram would have been far better. One could also wish that the graphics capabilities of the Apple, the only computer for which the program is currently available, were more refined. Still, life inside a schematic diagram need not be all that detailed, and the software's painless pedagogy and flexibility, which inspire truly imaginative problem solving, more than make up for the hardware's limitations.

One small constraint is placed upon the designer's style by the stipulation that the wiring, laid down with the soldering pen, be arranged in straight lines, a provision conducive to prim and proper engineering, but one that seems to slow down young designers. A lesser straitjacket on the imagination is the fact that wires cannot be stretched from room to room. Although no such feat is called for by the circumstances of the game, Genevieve and Tanya both had wild dreams of turning a whole series of rooms into a super-robot.

There is probably no one who has played computer games for any length of time who has not, on at least a few occasions, thought of creating a better one. But designing video games is an arcane art, since the secrets of its craftsmanship reside within the very machine code of the computer itself. Designing games not only requires consummate programming skills; it forces the creator to deal with the computer's capabilities on its own terms, in the most elementary particles of binary language, the zeroes and ones. It is an intellectual feat equivalent to batting .400.

However, for Apple owners, there exists an intermediary in the form of The Arcade Machine, from Broderbund Software, a package that lets you create your own video games without knowing how to program at all. Of course, the ease with which even novices are enabled to develop their own game concepts is bound to entail a tradeoff somewhere. What is sacrificed is range. The possibilities for pictorial expansion and complexity of play are limited, and the overall involvement of the would-be designer is far less than it is in Robot Odyssey I. The end results are inevitably confined to those shoot-'em-down or gobble-'em-up visuals that, in the space of a mere couple of years, became, for better or worse, one of the greatest cultural forces among the male youth of the Western world.

The program itself is menu driven. That is, the user is presented with lists of choices from which to select such options as creating shapes, paths, or explosions, or picking colors. Whan a particular design segment is completed, the user returns to the main menu to make another selection, and so on.

The initial designing of a game centers on a miniprogram within The Arcade Machine called the shape creator, which contains sequences allowing you to create visual images, referred to as aliens, in up to four colors plus black and white, the spectral limitations imposed on your imagination by the hardware. Once designed, these creatures are fixed in appearance and are not altered by playing.

The miniprogram also creates so-called explosions, which result from a confrontation between one of these aliens and a missile, whose design is also provided for by the software. Tanks are the objects to be controlled by the player. They will fire the missiles.

The shapes themselves are not limited to the visual representations called to mind by their code names. My kids like to create catlike creatures with wiggly tails as their aliens. I say they are catlike because the Apple's screen resolution is not fine enough to allow for the design of a truly recognizable

77

feline. Nevertheless, imagination is a wonderful thing, and hidden in the proud exclamation "Look, Dad, there's *our* shape! Isn't it neat?" probably lies mental imagery no less fanciful than that conjured up by my reading of Hans Christian Andersen when I was a child.

A second section of the program, the path creator, displays two rectangles defining the playing field, along with a set of crosshairs. By manipulating the crosshairs, the designer constructs a path table, a series of commands directing the future action of the shapes. Moving the crosshairs is like moving one of those robot arms that, once guided through a task by human hands, remembers the sequence of movements involved and is capable of repeating them.

Not only are the paths for the shapes to follow variable along the points of a crude compass rose, but the speed of their movement can be altered as well. During the construction of a game, the vertical and horizontal coordinates of an object are continuously displayed on the lower part of the screen, so a designer subconsciously develops a sense of this particular small segment of mathematics.

Some fairly sophisticated variations are possible. A time limit, ranging from a trigger-happy one second to a full hour and forty minutes, can be imposed on each play. Target scores may be varied as well. One can assign a value of from zero to 990 points to shooting down a bomb, for example. Bombs may also be made to bounce off certain targets. Scoring can be matched to the difficulty levels of the game.

Designing a game utilizing all these features takes a considerable amount of time. Luckily, there is also a load save feature, as it is called, so one can take time out from one's endeavors to eat and sleep and make copies of the finished masterpiece. A particularly appealing shape or background, once completed, can also be merged with a new game. It is possible, in other words, to develop a building-block library of game parts to be put together whenever and however you want.

The sound section of The Arcade Machine offers only a narrow selection, and the instructions are less than clear. However, a little experimentation soon has the player creating a limited number of sonic disturbances. Other options include a choice between one player and two as well as a range of background variations and possible missile trajectories.

From my daughters' point of view, the sound segment of the software was its weak point. One can go only so far in orchestrating explosions and missiles. The capability to compose even simple melodic refrains without harmony would be a great addition to the program, as would be the ability to construct more complex shapes.

In the short span of time since computer games first captured the devoted interest of American youth, their graphics have progressed from the crude paddles and light ball of the early Pong to the at least childlike complexity of Pac-Man and the various space invaders. To a great extent, the artistic limitations of The Arcade Machine are a product of Apple's less than refined graphics abilities, and reflect the state of the art in computer graphics today. As visual display in personal computer technology improves, a more aesthetically pleasing version of the software will no doubt appear. When it does, the game of game designing will become one that can be played almost forever. One could hope that, along with this development, a kindlier and more humane interest would supplant the more aggressive and warlike content of the games so dominant today.

Meanwhile, verbal-only games have also been translated into a personal computer format. Here pictures don't count. Here, too, intellectual skills gain ascendancy over the trigger-happy sleight of hand of motor-coordination contests.

Most such print-on-the-screen games are still back in the Pong age. A few, however, stand out as milestones on the road to sophistication. Among these sure signposts are Deadline, from Infocom, and that company's subsequent releases, Suspended, Sorcerer, Enchanter, The Witness, and so on.

Like those slightly bizarre "mystery weekends" now gaining in popularity throughout the land, during which you and fellow guests at a hotel or resort take part in a staged crime and then spend hours sorting through the clues trying to separate the actors from the real guests in order to determine

79

who committed the fictitious crime, these computer games are interactive. You take part in them and what you do affects what occurs. These games will give you days of challenge, frustration, and, eventually, pleasure.

Deadline comes in the form of a brown file folder stuffed with police, laboratory, and coroner's reports, a photograph of the scene of the crime, interviews, a casebook, and other clues for the would-be detective to peruse, as well as a disk for the waiting Watsonian computer. It is definitely a package to pique the curiosity of the murder-mystery lover. It certainly piqued mine.

So I loaded up the disk drive and found myself standing "on a wide lawn just north of the entrance to the Robner Estate." Making a tentative beginning, I typed in GO INTO HOUSE.

The computer responded, "There's no obvious way in from here."

I hadn't realized how sizable the Robner Estate was. Could have sworn I'd seen a large stone Tudor with a dark green door quite clearly in my mind. I typed in LOOK FOR FRONT DOOR.

The answer to that was, "You can't see any front door here."

How about GO UP THE PATH, then?

"You can't see any path here."

Looking about for Keep Off the Grass signs, as I was obviously standing on the lawn, I pecked in WALK NORTH.

That did it. I made my way to the door and proceeded to rap on it.

My knock was answered by Mrs. Robner herself, who in rather stilted English informed me of her grief and the fact that her husband's will would be read at noon should I care to attend. She then excused herself to get a bite to eat.

The computer clock indicated 8:03. It had taken me three minutes to come this far, and I was grateful that the digital display showed only the hour and the minutes, not elapsed seconds. The program had allotted me twelve hours in which to solve the murder. I had eleven hours and fifty-seven minutes left.

Perhaps the kitchen was the place to start. I typed in GO TO

80

THE KITCHEN, only to be told that I didn't know where it was. That was true enough.

FOLLOW MRS. ROBNER, I tried next. Peeking into the pantry, I found nothing more suspicious than the usual staples and canned goods.

Mrs. Rourke was in the kitchen cleaning up. Deciding to start my interrogation with her, I asked, MRS. ROURKE, WERE YOU HERE AT THE TIME OF MR. ROBNER'S DEATH?

"The word *time* can't be used," I was informed, "in that sense."

Since when?

Taking another tack with an obviously tough cookie, I queried, MRS. ROURKE, WHERE WERE YOU WHEN MR. ROBNER'S DEATH OCCURRED?

The answer was, "The word *when* isn't in your vocabulary."

That left me speechless. Whoever heard of a detective so deficient in vocabulary?

My mind turned momentarily to Mrs. Robner, who, according to her previously announced plan, was by now presumably dining. It suddenly seemed an admirable idea.

Removing myself momentarily from the scene of the crime, I made myself two hard-boiled egg and anchovy sandwiches on rye, mayonnaise on the egg side. Grabbing a Molson's red-label ale to wash them down with, I returned to the computer. Normally, I prefer cucumber sandwiches on thin pumpernickel as the appropriate accompaniment to a British mystery, but this one, set by transposition in my own back yard in Connecticut, obviously required something more fortifying.

Placing the ale and the sandwiches carefully at some distance from the computer, as is wise when introducing items of food and drink to the environs of these machines, I reached for that all-American last resort, the instructions. In the case of Deadline, these are quite specific, delineating the forms of movement available to me as a detective—up, down, north, south, and so on—and the way to use the stenographic service provided. Believe me, in this game it's handy to have a printer to produce hard copy of the queries for later reference. The instructions also showed me how to question suspects—

81

always politely, using each person's name the first time around. It needn't be Mr. or Mrs., first names would do if one knew them. But the name must be there in every initial query. Otherwise the computer wouldn't know which of the people in a room was being addressed.

Having finished scanning the instructions as well as devouring the sandwiches, I sternly pecked in, MRS. ROURKE, TELL ME ABOUT MR. ROBNER.

I was greeted with a flood of information about what a fine man he had been, how worried he had been about his business, and other matters in a similar vein. Mrs. Rourke commented on charity beginning at home. Of course, she remarked, she'd always been well treated.

DID HE TREAT MRS. ROBNER WELL?

"The word *did* is not in your vocabulary."

Like heck it isn't.

I stomped out, by entering GO NORTH—and ran right into what the computer informed me was a corner.

TURN LEFT.

"The word *left* isn't in your vocabulary."

I should have known.

GO WEST, I countered.

This put me in the dining room. After spending some time looking behind what appeared to be an original Seurat ("Nothing there.") and then behind all the other pictures ("There is nothing behind the [sic] all the pictures."), I endeavored to look out at the rose garden the software had assured me was there. My attempt was unsuccessful. So I made to leave the room, a departure not as easy as normal circumstances would allow.

In this game it is best to make a floor map of the house as one goes. As for the stenographic service, paper is a necessary adjunct to the screen. In fact, when all is said and done, probably more pages will be consumed by computer mysteries like Deadline than by the traditional "Slip them in your pocket and read them on the way to work" variety. The computerized mysteries may also require more thinking.

Deadline is so interactive that your movements around the house actually affect the outcome, as they might in real life.

If you do not reach a certain room before the housekeeper makes her regular rounds, for instance, she will clean away an important clue. It is even possible for a second murder to occur, if you don't stay on your toes. Furthermore, it's one of the few mysteries in which the detective—in this case you—may come to a bad end. Only logic and deduction in the best of the Sherlock Holmes/Nero Wolfe tradition will see you through.

Deadline is at one and the same time a crude harbinger of things to come and a rather amazing feat of state-of-the-art programming. If you read mysteries for relaxation, perhaps the game is not for you. If you read them to solve them, on the other hand, and if you don't mind dealing with the computer's understandably still less than perfect syntax, then Deadline and its siblings are very probably for you. Their ace serve is that there is absolutely no way to peek at the last page.

Effectively blocking the human temptation to turn to the answer page is one of the largest contributions made by the computer to puzzle-solving and verbal challenge games. Like mysteries, word games have a long and honorable tradition in Western culture, and as popular entertainment forms they were bound to have their bastions stormed by computer cursors sooner or later. Even the crossword puzzle eventually capitulated to computerization.

Some of the electronic crossword puzzles proliferating on screen are merely video versions of the traditional leisure-time activity. Others, such as Concentration Crosswords, from Science Research Associates, add a unique twist that only a computer can conveniently supply.

What sets Concentration Crosswords apart from ordinary crossword puzzles, aside from the fact that you cannot play it on the subway, unless you sport a very portable portable, is that it can be played by a single person or several. The software includes three separate games: Solitaire, for a single player; Key First, for up to four players or two teams of two; and Match Play, for two people taking turns.

Another thing separating this electronic crossword puzzle from its paper counterparts is that you have a choice between visible play and what is called a concentration version. In normal, or visible, play, words and letters correctly guessed remain on the screen as further reference points, following the usual crossword tradition. In the concentration mode, whenever you correctly identify a letter, the computer replaces it with an asterisk. This is definitely not the version for beginners.

There are fifty different puzzles in the Concentration Crosswords package, all of them challenging. Only one letter is in place on the nine-by-nine grid of squares at the start of play. Moreover, in a radical departure from traditional crossword puzzle presentation, no clues are provided. Straight guesswork is initially the order of the day. However, a hint option does permit you to have the machine fill in one other missing letter. I'd use it.

Adding to the challenge of Concentration Crosswords is the clock against which one plays, a silent timepiece situated at the upper right of the display. The seconds it registers slide away like the measured miles of an automobile odometer. A ticking version would be an improvement, adding a sense of urgency largely missing because one tends to keep one's eyes glued to the portion of the screen where the actual puzzle appears.

Cross Clues, for two players, another word game from Science Research Associates, uses a seven-by-seven grid but a more complex format than Concentration Crosswords. All the same, it is a faster game. In addition to the letters hidden in the grid, which surface as they are correctly guessed, there is a consonant bank that allows you a second chance on every turn. Pick a consonant after you have made your word guess, and it will appear wherever it belongs in the puzzle. A letter so appearing earns the player who selected it one point.

A variable time limit for each player allows the game to be tailored to participants of unequal skill. For example, a parent can be allotted, say, a one-minute time limit and a child a three-minute cutoff. Such flexibility is another factor, incidentally, that positively separates computer word games from their traditional counterparts.

On the other hand, it may be that computers penalize

adults, or at least adults new to computerized keyboards, cursor keys, and joysticks, by better accommodating the more nimble fingers of youth. For example, to enter a letter in Cross Clues, a player must move arrows along the puzzle's perimeter until they indicate the coordinate at which the letter is to be entered. The arrows then return to their original locations at the lower left and right corners of the grid. This homing function results in much clumsy maneuvering, since a player usually wants to guess a letter in the same location as the previous guess. Also, when a player is moving the arrows by using the repeat key, they all too easily glide right past one end of the grid and appear at the beginning again, which can be frustrating. Interestingly enough, younger players rarely seem to have any problems with this overshoot, which can probably be attributed to a more practiced video game hand.

The verbal skills demanded by Cross Clues seem to require participants of at least high-school age, although a certain amount of verbalistic leeway is provided by the time variable. More appropriate for the younger set, however, is the puzzle game Crypto Cube, from Design Ware, suggested for children aged eight and up.

Looking something like Rubik's Cube, Crypto Cube has hidden words on all of its planes. As projected on the computer's flat screen, only three sides of the cube are visible, but it can be electronically rotated so that the others are displayed.

There is no clock against which to race. This program's particular fillip is that a wrong guess penalizes you by subtracting points from your score.

Guessing the correct words is next to impossible without referring to a word list. However, just such a list is provided, at the press of the asterisk key, for each of the fifty puzzles in the package. This lexical feature adds complexity and simplicity to the game at one and the same time. New puzzles can be created at any time, using the Crypto Cube software, a provision that extends the game's playability almost infinitely.

Neither solitaire nor party game is Hayden Software's Word

Challenge, in which the computer alone is your opponent. The program feeds a 90,000-word vocabulary into your machine and then challenges you to find the words in a grid of letters. Each letter used must adjoin the next one in a word. For example, a three-by-three grid with the letters I, D, E in the first row, A, L, C in the second, and S, N, G in the third contains forty-five words, including snail, sail, sale, glanced. . . . That's one of the easy ones.

One market for computer word games it seems to me the publishers are sadly overlooking is that of our senior citizens. The challenge and the interactiveness these verbal games offer could provide the elderly, and particularly the visually handicapped, with hours of entertainment at an intellectual and social level far above that of televison viewing, if only they came in a large-type edition so as to be more legible. Between the television set and the personal computer monitor, we are all going to become a nation of myopes in any case, so there would be no dearth of prospective buyers for the magnified versions.

But enough of games, you say, as I did after playing through the suitcaseful of them I had brought home from the NCC. What else is there?

Well, would you believe a game for accountants? Actually, of course, it's not really a game. It's an electronic spreadsheet, a very serious piece of software indeed, one that is charting the future of numerous corporations, large and small, in this country today. Originally it was called VisiCalc, and it's the software that took personal computing from the children and put it on the desk of your stockbroker.

Now stockbrokers and accountants are very serious people. They don't play games. Certainly not with other people's money. Or do they?

6: "What If?" The Question That Launched a Million Micros

America has been classed, a little less than charitably, as a nation obsessed with numbers, and its reputation in this regard goes back some distance in time. As an English traveler, Thomas Hamilton, noted in 1833, arithmetic seemingly "comes by instinct among this guessing, reckoning, expecting, and calculating people."

While his observation may have been well founded, civilization's numeric fixation predates this country's formation by a considerable span of time, beginning when man first put pen to paper, or, I should say, stick to clay. The earliest known Sumerian tablets date from the golden commercial age, circa 3000 B.C., when some young whelp, no doubt, invented a quick cuneiform accounting system in the family chariot shed. They deal mostly with numbers—of sheep, tools, and urns, not to mention interest paid and taxes.

Mathematical means of reckoning underwent no radical

changes in the various commercial civilizations that followed. Oh, after nearly five thousand years one noticed that even small businesses had gone from scribe and clay tablet to pen and paper or even typewriter and paper. Also, when it came to redoing, say, a series of financial calculations because a lender had just raised the interest rate by half a point, throwing all the other figures out of whack, a bucket of whiteout could be observed to have replaced the clay compactor. Overall, however, the progress made in computation had been minimal.

Were it not for all the erasing and whiting out, juggling with figures, as in solving the puzzle of how to pay the absolute minimum amount of taxes possible, could be a game. It was the playful possibilities of figures that finally set the stage for the personal computer explosion. And although the explosion occurred on the West Coast, as anyone following the media hype about the new technomillionaires is more than well aware, the detonation occurred in Boston.

There a Harvard business student, Dan Bricklin, was running out of patience with erasers and whiteout while doing recalculation after recalculation of casebook financial budgets. Change one figure and, as likely as not, you'd have to change all the rest. There had to be a better way.

The better way turned out to be what is now known generically as electronic spreadsheet, or calc, software. Dan Bricklin and Robert Frankston wrote the program. Daniel Fylstra distributed it, through a small software company he had formed. The program was released in 1979 under the name VisiCalc. Initially, it ran on only one computer, the Apple.

In retrospect, it seems indisputable that VisiCalc is what took personal computing out of the playroom and planted it firmly in the middle of the office. What it did not do, however, was remove the gaming mentality from personal computing.

VisiCalc was certainly not sold as a game. It was sold as a utilitarian and quite serious tool, if one that was a little magical as well, to aid in answering the perennial "What if?" questions of business. What if I amortized the loan at 14 percent over fifteen years instead of 13 percent over twelve years? What if I deferred the purchase of the new equipment until next year's budget? What if I put three employees on overtime instead of hiring a new one?

It was so easy to ask the computer such questions, and so much fun to watch it send a ripple across the screen, changing all the numbers that needed to be changed to match the new entries. Then too, the results of its recalculations were so highly and quickly visible that they opened a whole new world of projections for financial analysts and others dealing much with interrelated sums or measures. Work once shunted off to lesser accountants and draftsmen, or else avoided altogether, became a main attraction for the executives and visionaries of the numerical world.

VisiCalc could, and often did, hook anyone who came near its magic. Spreadsheets began to be used for any task that could be entered in a row and column format. Straight profit and loss accounting gave way to regression and correlation analysis and other creative statistical manipulations. Spreadsheets made number crunching a pleasure.

As the business community began buying personal computers and spreadsheet software, mutual aid societies known as users' groups began to spring up for aficionados of VisiCalc and, later, the even more feature-filled Lotus 1-2-3. Excited about their own experiences, but also eager to learn of new applications others had discovered for the programs, and in truth often snagged on a problem with the software here or there, the converts to on-screen number crunching began to convene.

The clubhouse is central to many a childhood. Its rudimentary walls might be no fancier than nailed-together scraps from equipment crates and pallets reminiscent of a Norman Rockwell painting, complete with a No Girls Allowed plaque over the door. Later its structure might be replaced by the sorority or fraternity house, or merely the invisible enclosure of a clique. But the prerequisite to membership in the club would remain the same: a shared secret.

Personal computing in its infancy was also a clubhouse conventicle, open only to the neophyte guided by friends through the ornate initiation rites of digital electronics. What is perhaps surprising is that clubbiness among computer owners remains in evidence to this day, even as mass marketing and advertising are well-nigh promoting a feeling of guilt in anyone stalwart enough to have resisted the siren of Silicon Valley and thus to have become, according to the hype, perhaps the last person in America not to possess or be possessed by a personal computer. Yet in this instance, and particularly in the case of the novice computer owner, the clubbiness is all to the good.

Personal computer clubs are probably one of the best and least painful ways for a beginner to find out what to do with his computer. Their meetings, bulletin boards, and newsletters, often replete with announcements, special requests, opinion columns, and software reviews, can provide valuable pointers for the novice.

Computer club meetings are a lot less intimidating than the machines themselves. The membership of a New York IBM PC Users' Group meeting I attended was a rather comforting amalgam of human beings. A standing-room-only crowd of three-piece-suited businessmen and executive women, bearded, blue-jeaned computer freaks, and a smattering of youngsters packed the hall in supportive camaraderie.

First on the agenda of the session I visited was a hardware report, which began with the comment, "Half a mo, actually, I have to make a telephone call," followed by the disappearance of the speaker. The treasurer's report ensued, then an announcement concerning the formation of "a group for people who have no experience with computers or the IBM PC."

When the hardware reporter returned to center stage, one of the reasons for belonging to a users' group became obvious. His account covered the wheeling and dealing he had been doing, buying equipment, such as memory boards and modems to connect computers to the telephone system, at sizable discounts from their list prices, for the New York PC members.

There were numerous other reports, on graphics, data base management, and new club software. Recently developed programs were available from the club on more than half a dozen diskettes, each selling for only $6, an obvious bargain whose value was confirmed when I joined a long winding

90

queue during the midsession break for what I thought was the water fountain, only to discover after ten minutes in line that everyone was waiting to purchase club software, not to quench his thirst.

Following the various reports, the meeting was opened to members' questions and comments.

"Does anyone have any experience operating the PC as a cash register?"

"I'm interested in starting a special interest group for communications."

"For those who asked about the QB keyboard at the last meeting, it works fine."

"I'm interested in doing PC consulting."

"You think the automobile companies make a lot of recalls! I don't know what's the matter with IBM. . . ."

There was plenty of discussion about updates and upgrades. Good humor and a certain mutual commiseration over the more aggravating aspects of personal computing prevailed, making both the novice and the experienced computerist feel at home.

There's no disputing the fact that a gathering of people as diverse in experience as the members of a computer users' group are bound to be will leave the first-timer in a state of some confusion. The uninitiated cannot help but feel lost when someone asks, "Is anyone doing 3780 emulations?"

Still, the flavor of it all is perhaps summed up by the response of the New York PC group to the query put forth by the club's chairman, Joe Rigo, in leading the meeting I attended: "Where are the beginners? Every month the beginners come up to me and say, 'I didn't understand a thing.' So where are the beginners?"

Hesitantly they began to stand up. "I'm a beginner. . . ."

Thunderous applause greeted each admission, followed by an almost revival-meeting-like acceptance of the newcomer into the group. There were plenty of offers of help from the more experienced club members.

Among the benefits the New York PC group provided its members was a regular lecture series. Two talks were given the evening I visited the club, one on PC maintenance programs, the other on business graphics. Future topics to be covered included tax considerations for PC owners, PCs that talk, PCs that understand speech, and software for the home.

Surprisingly enough, the home, too, is being invaded by those versatile spreadsheets that so captivated the business community. On the home front one doesn't find the complex do-it-all calc programs, such as SuperCalc and EasyCalc, which can take six months to conquer, nor Symphony, Lotus's successor to 1-2-3, which some wags claim is a lifelong learning experience, but rather very specialized spreadsheets designed with a single purpose in mind—beating the tax man at his own game.

It could not honestly be said that programs such as The Personal Tax Planner, from Aardvark/McGraw-Hill, or Tax Preparer, from Howard Soft, make paying taxes fun. They do, however, turn the drudgeries of tax time into a strategy game in which the IRS becomes an opponent a little less overbearing than usual.

The Personal Tax Planner and Tax Preparer both perform as other spreadsheets do. But all the preliminary work of setting up the framework into which the numbers are to be plugged has been done for you. Also, since the rules in the IRS game are not constant, and never a year goes by without some change being made in the tax laws, annual updates of the software are made available, their price depending on the complexity that particular year's sitting of Congress has bestowed upon them. All these expenditures, by the way, along with part of the cost of your computer, should themselves be tax deductible, just as the more traditional expenses of tax preparation routinely are.

Exactly what do these tax planners do? They allow you to fiddle almost endlessly with your tax return in order to minimize what you must pay. Please note that you are fiddling with the return, which is perfectly legal. You are not fiddling with the taxes themselves. There's a lot more flexibility in tax accounting than meets the eye. That's why there are so many attorneys in the field.

Being myself in a profession where the income is irregular, to say the least, I have used an electronic tax planner to good advantage. For example, I entered the second half of the advance for this book, which will come as a lump sum, into a tax planning program to test two possible payment plans for it. My question was, would I be better off taking the money this year, and then income averaging, or would it cause me less agony at tax time to postpone the second advance payment until next year? Contrary to my expectations, income averaging turned out to be the alternative that would let me keep more money. Postponing the payment would give the IRS more than its due—a lot more, in fact, than the combined cost of the program and the computer.

For those who have a "regular job," as my mother, who has a great deal of difficulty recognizing writing as a form of employment, would put it, one of the most common fluctuations in income affecting personal tax returns is a gain or loss incurred by selling stocks or a house or other tangible goods. When and how you sell can make a big difference in the taxes you pay.

Let's say that it's the end of the year and you have a potential $2,000 profit on your shares of United Cat and Dog. Let's also say that lately the stock has not been performing as well as it had been doing before. Unfortunately, there's a month yet to go before that $2,000 profit becomes a long-term capital gain. If you sell now, you will have to treat it as a short-term gain and pay much higher taxes on it. What should you do?

Using, say, The Personal Tax Planner, you can call up its alternatives mode and fill out a worksheet on the computer screen with all the usual tax gobbledygook, including your filing status, exemptions, wages, and so on. Then you can set up the variable or variables affecting your taxes, in this case your $2,000 profit. In one column you would enter the $2,000 as your potential long-term gain should the stock keep its current price for another month. In the next column you would enter the $2,000 as the short-term gain you would invite if you were to sell the stock tomorrow. In the third column you would enter, say, $1,800; in the fourth, $1,500; and in the fifth, $1,200. These figures, all coming under the heading of a long-term gain, would represent your estimates of how much the stock might decline over the following month.

93

Press the *R* key for results, and the computer screen will light up, simply to let you know that something is happening rather than leaving you staring at a blank screen, with "Starting Tax Calculations," followed by "Now Doing Tax Calculations," "Finishing Tax Calculations," and, in less than a minute, "Calculations Completed." At this point, the computer will display, simultaneously, five different sets of data showing you how much the taxes would be in each of the hypothetical cases you have projected.

The process sounds more complex than it is. The Personal Tax Planner is a relatively simple program to use. Furthermore, it is capable of automatically taking all kinds of variables into account, including income averaging, the self-employment tax, business income, IRA and Keogh payments, and so on. If you have been putting $1,000 a year aside in an IRA, might it pay to put in nothing this year and $2,000 next year, because you're expecting a raise in six months? Would husband and wife be better off filing separate returns or filing jointly? What effect would the interest on a car loan have on your taxes if you were to buy the vehicle next year instead of this year? Would it pay to rent a house instead of buying one?

In addition to the alternatives mode, both The Personal Tax Planner and Tax Preparer have a projection mode. Let's say your wife has been staying home raising the children for a number of years, but is now planning to go back to work. How would the second salary affect your taxes? Would there even be anything left at all after expenses and taxes? To put it another way, what would the second salary have to amount to in order to be worthwhile? The tax planning programs answer such questions effortlessly.

The software allows you to see the tax implications of almost any financial decision you can think of. The computer games you can play with the IRS are endless, although the results of the software's manipulations are only as good as your guesses as to what your income stream will be.

The differences between the two software packages have to do primarily with their ease of use and the distance they cover in carrying you toward the preparation of your final tax return. Aardvark's Personal Tax Planner adopts the number mentality so predominant in computing—and so difficult, not to mention off-putting, for people accustomed to dealing with real words and real people rather than with numerical representations and unresponsive machines. The filing status line, for example, contains the familiar litany of headings offered by the IRS, the categories *Single, Married Filing Joint Return, Head of Household,* and so on. But instead of typing in your status, you enter the number 1, 2, or 7, respectively. These numbers in no way match the corresponding checkoffs on the 1040 form. The program also omits commas when dealing with large numbers. A $30,000 salary, say, is entered as 30000. This convention, both inconvenient and unfamiliar to the ordinary taxpayer, is highly conducive to the introduction of errors.

Howard Soft's Tax Preparer does use commas, so one can enter $30,000 in the customary way, something which alone might tempt me to choose it over the competition. Even so, the program can be confusing, in part because it follows the IRS's way of doing things. Ideally, a tax planner should be set up to handle information in whatever way you do, and then to translate it automatically, when all the computations are completed, into the proper format for the IRS.

The largest difference between the two programs, however, is probably not to be found in the format they use, but in the separate approaches their very titles imply. The Personal Tax Planner provides you with all the tools you need in order to juggle the figures to minimize your taxes. The Tax Preparer does that too, but it also prints out your final return in a form acceptable to the IRS. Whether this is a feature you need depends on how seriously you take programs of this sort.

I find them helpful for planning and setting up the figures so that my attorney does not have to plow through my annual shoeboxes of receipts. However, the final say I leave to her, and the forms to her firm's large computer. I feel uncomfortable playing software in a world where the IRS plays hardball.

One aspect of spreadsheets in general that has always made me feel uncomfortable is that they seem to require as their adjuncts, in my case, at any rate, a calculator and a note pad and pencil. Surely one should not need so many extra pieces cluttering up a desk already overflowing with computer components and the other detritus of tabletop thinking. One of the more incongruous aspects of personal computing, in fact, has been that most people using a calc package, with all its built-in arithmetic, trigonometric, and statistical functions, have needed at least a calculator at their side as well. Here is all this raw number-crunching power, and the machine can't multiply 236 by 4,232 for you.

Actually, to be strictly accurate, one would have to say that it is possible to induce the computer to multiply the figures for you. But until very recently that meant dumping the program you were running and then loading special, separate calendar/calculator/notebook software to do the job.

Now, however, there are available a number of runalong programs designed to serve just such auxiliary functions not handled by the calc programs themselves. Three of the leading contenders for this associative role are Sidekick, from Borland International, the Desk Organizer, from Warner Software, and Spotlight, from Software Arts.

A runalong program sidles into your computer's memory and sits there in the background waiting for you to summon it forth. When you do so, the main program you are running is put temporarily into a state of suspended animation. Once you are through with your subsidiary calculations or note scribbling or both, you are returned to the original program at exactly the point where you left it. The calculations you take with you, entering them wherever desired.

Sidekick is the most basic of the three runalong programs mentioned above. It pops up on screen when you press the control and the alternate keys simultaneously, presenting you with a choice of Notepad, Calculator, Calendar, Dialer, ASCII Table, Help, and Setup. The last two alternatives you won't need after you have run the program once or twice. The ASCII Table is pertinent only for programmers. The others do just what you may have been hoping they would do. They make life with the computer a little easier.

They also take up some extra memory, which is something you may not have been counting on. Let's say you have a computer with 256K of built-in RAM memory. You are running Lotus 1-2-3, which really needs all of those 256K to run well. Where do you put Sidekick, which requires 20K to 100K or even more, depending on what you are using it for, or Spotlight, which requires a minimum of 75K? You guessed it. You end up buying more internal memory—remember my earlier contention that you never have enough of that commodity—usually in the form of a second memory board to insert in one of the computer's expansion slots so thoughtfully provided by the manufacturer, who just knew that you would eventually want to double up to 512K.

Doubling up is becoming as common in our culture as the Doublemint twins. The two-car family is nearly established as a standard, as are the two-bathroom and the two-television-set homes. The new cooking ranges have two ovens, and most sinks are double. This twofer consumerism may well be a minor indication of temporary market saturation. After all, the necessity of such duality is, in most cases, doubtful. Two of a kind may be convenient, yes, but how often are they really essential?

The latest duplex question is directed specifically to first-time computer buyers. Most of them are not yet faced with the question of which second computer to buy, although that too is a probable eventuality. Nor does add-on memory pose a real dilemma in most instances. No, the question at the moment is whether to purchase one disk drive or two.

In the case of a Kaypro, a Northstar, or some other machine with two disk drives built right in, the choice has obviously been made for you. But when it comes to such popular personal computers as the Apple II series, the Commodore, IBM's PCjr, the Macintosh, or Radio Shack's TRS-80, you will have to make the decision yourself. It's a rather important decision, too, because one disk drive may cost more than two low-priced computers.

So how do you decide, especially when the computer salesman makes owning a second disk drive seem as natural as having two hands? The answer, like that to almost all questions having to do with the options available in computerland, is based on what you intend to use the computer for.

The Apple IIe I have is equipped with two disk drives, but

I don't use the second one very often. My family uses the Apple primarily as either a game machine or an electronic tutor, running recreational or instructional programs on it. Neither function really requires a second disk.

However, one area—and a common one in computing—where a second disk drive becomes a very handy accessory indeed is that of copying. Here the second drive can virtually be considered a computer's private duplicating machine.

It's all too easy to destroy a disk. Of course, no one would ever drink coffee or soda while working at a computer terminal. But if someone happened to do so, and if someone just happened to spill a bit of either of those sticky beverages on a disk, it would be bye-bye to whatever information was stored on that disk. You can't dry out a floppy as you do a book subjected to a similar misfortune, prying the volume apart and reading through the stains darkly.

Human error does not alone shoulder the responsibility for destroyed disks. Computers are fabled for their sudden impulse to "eat" a disk or mangle its data. It doesn't happen very often. The occurrence is usually limited to the one time you have no backup disk.

Thus the convenience of having a second disk drive so that you can copy data from one disk to another at regular intervals as you work usually justifies the purchase all by itself. It is feasible to make backups with a single drive. But under such circumstances, human nature being what it is, copying often loses the race with procrastination.

For word processing, the advantages of a second drive far exceed its convenience in simply copying. It is possible, for example, to keep a whole library of pat paragraphs and boilerplate matter stored on the second disk. As you write on the first disk, you can call up any of these preboiled phrases that apply and insert them at will, within the flash of a second, in your current composition. The repetitive drudgery of typing form letters is also immediately obviated by a second drive. (It is unfortunate that the boredom of receiving such letters cannot be likewise obliterated.)

Where a second disk drive may become less an option than a true necessity is in the running of electronic spreadsheets.

Multiplan, from Microsoft, will run with only one disk drive. Lotus 1-2-3 and The Incredible Jack, from Business Solutions, on the other hand, cannot operate on a computer so configured.

If, after weighing its advantages, you decide that a second disk drive is right for your computer, your next choice will be between simply another floppy drive and a hard disk, sometimes called a Winchester, supposedly so named because IBM, which developed the technology, first used the product code 3030, recalling the Winchester .30-.30 rifle of the Old West. A hard disk adds a great deal of convenience and a tremendous amount of memory capacity to a computer system, though at a considerable cost compared to that of a second floppy.

The trend, however, is toward including a hard disk in the basic computer unit. Texas Instruments' Professional and IBM's AT, for example, as well as the older IBM XT, on which this book is being edited, are hard disk driven. Because of this, I can switch almost instantly from word processing to a spelling checker, Sidekick's calculator, or an outlining program such as Think Tank. They are all stored on the hard disk for quick access.

If, at some other time, I happen to be working with a really large spreadsheet of thirty or forty columns, I can summon Sideways, from Funk Software, to rotate the printout ninety degrees so that the printed copy of my calculations is churned out sideways. For all that program cares, you could have hundreds of columns to your spreadsheet, although if you also had hundreds of rows, you would still have to do some cutting and pasting.

For someone like myself, unaccustomed to much dealing with large spreadsheets, the thought of one several hundred columns wide by several thousand rows long is mind boggling. But that's just where the calc programs seem to be taking the faithful of numeracy. At one time 255 rows was considered a substantial spreadsheet. Then Lotus 1-2-3 allowed for over 2,000 rows. SuperCalc 3, from Sorcim, now lets you enter data in 9,000 rows.

The more space there is for data to spread out in, the more

information people seem to find to be processed. It may well be that, only five years after their birth, electronic spreadsheets are reaching a size where they are handling more information than they ought to be allowed to deal with.

As spreadsheets increase in size, the scope of decisions based on their results naturally increases as well. Now surfacing are reports of multimillion-dollar errors caused by poorly designed setups and oversights in spreadsheet models for accounting and projections. The wholesale adoption of spreadsheets has led to a gospel-in-printout mentality among far too many people. The classic old dictum, *Garbage In, Garbage Out,* is truer than ever as the dumps increase in size. Yet simply because more people are entering more garbage into more computers, a new-found sense of power instilled by the modern marvel of swift and efficient electronic processing often leads to an acceptance of the reassuring printouts at face value, even when a gnawing doubt spawned by instinct should make one think twice.

It is all too easy to be inconsistent in applying the rules of normal accounting to an expansive spreadsheet. An applicable price discount can be included for one product line and inadvertently omitted for another in a company's financial projections, for example. It is also all too easy to use a model for, say, projected sales that is quite unwittingly flawed. The problem then becomes one of error detection. In such instances, even if a mistake is discovered, which is a big if, it may be impossible to rectify.

I have no doubt but that spreadsheets will cost this nation's businesses losses in the millions. This is not to say that commerce will fail to gain much more by the use of such software. But a world enthusiastically storming the future needs to add a little balance to the particular perspective offered by new tools. Why, even software as harmless, uncontroversial, and obviously beneficial as word processing first appears to be can have unexpectedly adverse repercussions.

7: Where Have You Gone, Noah Webster?

What electronic spreadsheets did to spread the personal computer gospel among businessmen, word processing did for the public at large. Reporters, writers, and editors, the people who create the news, if not its content, were enthralled by the concept. Here was a new tool that could make the verbal life easier, faster paced, even exhilarating.

With the media enraptured by word processing, personal computers were bound to become part and parcel of the feature-story-writing set. How could one resist describing in glowing terms something that professed to liberate one from the tedium of the typewriter? Never mind that most people were not writers. They were going to love word processors. A flowering of people's literature, a renaissance of letters, was just around the keyboard. Today, asked what they expect to do with a personal computer, almost 75 percent of those who indicate that they expect to do anything at all with one mention word processing.

It is not surprising, then, that the question people inevitably ask me when they discover I am a writer is, "Which word processor do you use?"

My reply is unfailing and unabashed. "Narrow-lined yellow paper and an inexpensive ballpoint." The words are almost invariably greeted with either disbelief or scorn. Nevertheless, they embody the very essence of choosing a word processing package, for if it's not right for you, it's not right.

This is not to say that my words are never "processed." When it comes to the final draft, electronic polishing plays its part. But the original writing is done in a more traditional fashion for two reasons.

First of all, I write in odd places and at odd times. A crucial thought is apt to speed unexpectedly through my mind in the late-night darkness of our bedroom, in the barn while tending the livestock, in the canoe as I am coaxing a Tiny Torpedo surface lure between islands of lily pads, beneath one of which I know lurks a lunker bass. These are all environs not yet capable of being comfortably computerized.

The second reason has to do with my rather oddball method of actually putting words to paper. As many as twenty of those narrow-lined yellow pads may litter the table adjoining my desk, and I have been known to work, in the space of a few hours, on as many articles or book chapters as there have been pads laid out.

Granted, both of these limitations are self-imposed, not to mention being rather unusual. Interestingly enough, however, recent software developments are leading toward the design of word processing programs that might eventually overcome such restraints. At the same time, word processing is going from the generic to the specific in its application.

Once upon a time, long, long ago, say around 1979 or 1980, word processing software for personal computers, a brand-new phenomenon, tried to be everything to everyone. WordStar, from MicroPro, has been on the Softsel Hot List, a compilation of distributors' shipments to some 6,500 stores nationwide, almost since the inception of that ranking.

WordStar has an awful lot of bells and whistles built into it, featuring options like decimal alignment for arranging columns of numbers, slow screen scrolling of a whole document so you can just sit back and read, letting the computer "turn the pages" for you, and the ability to select from a variety of colored ribbons for printing.

However, it also has a 500-page manual that takes the average first-time computerist more weeks to plow through than a cat has lives. The on-screen control commands are not much easier to deal with. Slow screen scrolling, for example, is activated by a command that involves pressing the control key, then Q, then Q again, then control, then Z, then 9. Any Evelyn Woods graduate could have finished reading the document by the time all those keys had been pressed. Add to this the fact that a computer screen displaying WordStar processing in the works appears to be covered with chicken tracks of specialized command symbols, and that the vast majority of people probably use only 10 percent of WordStar's capabilities, and one can't help but wonder why the program is so popular.

The answer lies in the sociology of software. Apart from the pricing factor, the marketing of software is really not all that different from the purveying of other consumer products. WordStar happened to arrive on the personal computer scene at exactly the right time, just when sales of micros were beginning to take off and early potential buyers were trying to figure out what to do with them.

Largely because of its timely arrival, it also became ingrained in the salesmen's routines. After all, once you have dealt with the agonies of learning such a complex word processing program, it would take an awful lot to convince you to go through such a baptism by fire again. It's much easier simply to keep selling a product you can already look knowledgeable about. The fact that WordStar retailed for $495 and offered better-than-average profit margins was not exactly discouraging to salesmen either.

Because the program is so difficult to conquer, a host of

books designed to aid the new user were written about it, adding a bit of perverse psychology to the scene. Although very often these volumes were not much clearer than the program's incomprehensible manual itself, the very existence of a whole library of WordStar literature gave establishment imprimatur to the product.

In the same vein, some of the earliest converts to word processing were writers, who were understandably enamored of the idea of a machine doing their tedious retyping for them. WordStar became their de facto standard simply by being there. Asked what word processing software they used, the pioneers usually answered, "WordStar." So neophytes bought the same. That way they had mentors to turn to for help in trying to penetrate their new endeavor.

Thus a dinosaur was created. And like a dinosaur, WordStar is headed for extinction. Although it may well take a generation of word processors for that to come to pass, a software generation is only three or four years.

Overall, the acquisition of word processing skills still involves a frenzy of frustration lasting anywhere from several weeks to several months, depending on one's daily tolerance to torture. Furthermore, it requires an acceptance of Orwellian newspeak, however appropriate to our age that adjustment might be.

I well remember watching Susan struggling, as a first-timer, with the manual accompanying the Leading Edge word processing program. After several hours of trying to take advantage of the software's so-called automatic pagination feature, she had still failed to get any numbers on her pages. Typically, the manual, the cue cards, the tutorial, and the telephone help service, though always friendly and encouraging, had not been able to agree on the required steps. Finally she discovered that the company had redefined pagination to mean simply "dividing a document into unnumbered pages...." Never mind that by Webster's definition and according to all the rest of the world it means "the act of numbering the pages of a book, etc."

Computer manuals in general are so incomprehensible and devoid of meaning that most software companies have installed a telephone hot line so that users can reach them in case of problems. Some firms utilize an 800 number, and while I certainly would not make this provision the sole criterion in choosing a word processing package, I would hypothesize that without a toll-free help number, one could run up a telephone bill exceeding the cost of the software, which is not so inexpensive to begin with.

Talking to some people on the answering end of one of these lifelines, I was interested to learn that while almost everyone complains about the inadequacy of computer and software manuals, or documentation, the criticism falls into two diametrically opposed categories. The average user finds the manuals for the most part too complex. The techies and the more experienced users generally claim that they are not detailed enough. The necessity for a bifurcation of instructions to suit these two groups is something that software publishers are on the verge of discovering.

More and more programs are being released with interactive on-disk tutorials, accompanied in some cases by tape cassettes. Yet individual software publishers have themselves been surprisingly slow to pick up on this trend, to the extent that companies specializing exclusively in tutorials for the better-known programs have sprung up and prospered. Within a couple of years, perhaps, you may be able to pick up a word processing package and learn how to use it without ever reading a manual. The perusal of said handbook can then be left to the computer fanatic. The rest of us can use the volume to prop the monitor up at an angle, or for some other suitable purpose.

Typical of word processing software accompanied by its own on-disk tutorial is the Bank Street Writer, published by Broderbund. The Bank Street Writer is so easy to learn that my daughter Genevieve and her friend Joanna, both sixth graders at the time, conquered the basics of word processing in less than an hour using this software.

The on-disk tutorial covers the main functions of the program with enough clarity to be an introduction to the field of word processing itself. The first section explains text entering, capitalization, the use of the return key, and the wraparound feature, which allows you to keep typing past the end of a line and have the computer move the excess words onward, to the beginning of the next line. Replacing the carriage return on a typewriter, the wraparound is a basic word processing essential. So is the provision for capitalization and lowercasing of words.

For computers such as the Apple IIe and IIc and the IBM PC, the shift key is used in the normal fashion to elicit capitals. The old Apple II, however, taken alone, is an impossible choice for word processing, since it uses an all-capitals display. Circumventing this computer's limitations, Bank Street Writer gives it both upper and lower case. The user is required to strike the shift key, then the N key (whose shifted position ordinarily yields a caret), and only then the letter needing to be capitalized—not an elegant solution, but one that works. One soon learns to integrate striking shifts and carets into an automatic simultaneous move similar to the shift lock action used on a standard typewriter.

The introductory section of the Bank Street Writer tutorial also demonstrates the erase and unerase features, as they are called, of the software. The program is fairly forgiving; if you want to erase a whole block of text, it will let you do so, but first it will highlight the text in question and, before allowing you to finally pull the plug, query, "Are you sure you want to erase highlighted text?"

Move and move back commands are provided to allow the user to shift blocks of text back and forth as a unit within the whole text, using the same highlighting and query display. However, the maximum number of lines that can be moved at a time is fifteen. If there are twenty lines to be shifted, they must be moved in two blocks. In addition, the move back feature, which is used to return the text to its original location, works only on the last block moved. You'll have to do some extra juggling if you are prone to changing your mind in large matters.

Then again, Bank Street Writer is not one of the so-called full-feature word processing packages. Neither is Software Publishing's PFS:Write, the program I happen to use for editing. It is a little more complex than Bank Street Writer, but not much so.

A member of a family that also includes PFS:Graph, for simple graphics, and PFS:File, a data base management system, PFS:Write is geared for reasonably extensive use in small- to medium-sized businesses. Where the program really comes into its own is in its ability to interact with the other programs to create those resplendent documents replete with charts and tables that seem to dominate the world of commerce. The recent addition to the family of a compatible communications package, PFS:Access, extends the applications of the program even further. PFS:Proof, one of the fastest spelling checkers available, simplifies the proofreading of documents produced by this family of software.

PFS:Write does have some drawbacks eliminated in the more complex and inclusive word processing packages. For example, students contemplating research papers should be apprised that it is unable to combine double- and single-spaced text on the same page, except by the expedient of the writer's single-spacing and then manually inserting extra returns. It is also unable to start its automatic pagination without putting a physical number on the first page, in contradiction of proper manuscript style. In addition, it has a relatively short document length, though one longer than Bank Street's, and an inability to move blocks of type over a hundred lines or so in length in one step.

On the other hand, some of the criticisms of PFS:Write seem to be the product of writers who feel that if something isn't complex, it isn't good. For instance, a recent review characterized the program as "the obvious lightweight choice for someone who writes letters and nothing else." The review then went on to note that it was not possible to link files when printing, a function equivalent to writing separate chapters and then asking the computer to print them all out together, as in a book. Such a feat is patently possible with PFS:Write. Witness this book, the entire manuscript of which was edited and printed out using PFS:Write.

Trying to winnow the chaff from the grain in word processors by merely reading the reviews of them is an endeavor doomed to failure. There are already several hundred different word processing programs on the market, and no one is going to be familiar with all, or even most, of them, especially in view of their diversity and the complexity of so many of them.

The reason why so many word processing packages exist is twofold. First, the style and goals of programmers differ. Second, different users want different features. To delineate all the factors that ought to be taken into account in choosing word processing software would be impossible. The generality of such an attempt would negate quite valid individual preferences. But a start can be made, at least, on some of the basic features a good word processing program should have, provided one remembers that, as in the case of choosing an automobile, where I might prefer a 1951 MG TD and my neighbor a Ford LTD, the fundamentals to look for may be the same, but personal taste is the final arbiter.

The only way to test the roadability of a car is to take it for a spin. The only way to test the processability of a word processor is to run some words through it. By that I mean not merely an alternating couple of lines of "The quick brown fox jumped . . ." and "Now is the time for all good men . . . ," but a real honest-to-goodness document, as it is called in computerese. What you need is something at least a couple of thousand words long, or some seven or eight double-spaced pages, to give you a feel for the various capabilities of the software. It's helpful to have friends who use word processors you can try. Some stores will let you really test out what you are thinking of buying, because it saves them, as well as you, problems in the future. Other retailers adopt a "Take it and leave your money" attitude. Many of the latter seem, not surprisingly, to be closing their doors.

Once you have entered your test document into a word processing system, composed of a particular personal computer and its appropriate software, test the general ease of use of the various editing features, then measure the time it takes to execute the following four moves.

First, scroll from the beginning of the document to the end, one line at a time. Think of the document as a continuous roll of film. When you request the computer to scroll the text, the "film" will rise from the bottom of the screen and wind up at the top. Record how long it takes to do so.

Secondly, measure the time it takes to scroll from the beginning of the document to the end, one page, instead of one line, at a time.

Next, check to see how long you must wait for the cursor to advance from start to finish when you press the end key or otherwise command it to go to the end of the document.

Finally, hold down a key to repeat its character a hundred times, and clock that.

Raw speed isn't everything, but it is important, particularly once you have become adroit at handling the software. The miracles of word processing soon become minor when you must wait around for the machine to perform them.

Convenience in editing is, in a sense, another function of speed. For example, if three keystrokes are needed to switch from one preset margin to another in one word processing system and seven keystrokes are required to perform the same task in another system, the former may well be the preferred package for applications calling for frequent margin changes. When it comes to deleting characters, your choice in editing styles will consist mainly of opting for a special function key provided for the specific purpose of deleting characters or settling for striking the control key and then, say, the G key to make the deletion, using two strokes instead of one.

Such idiosyncrasies of word processors are for you to evaluate in terms of your own personal comfort or discomfiture and your own application requirements, balanced, of course, by considerations of price. One factor that is important whatever the style of the software, however, is the consistency of its command structure. Another is the display format.

When you type a page on a typewriter, what you see is what you get. This is not necessarily true in the case of a word processor. For a so-called screen-oriented word processing program, such as Leading Edge or Lifetree Software's Volkswriter Deluxe, the principle still holds true. In the case of a character-oriented program, such as PeachText, from Peachtree Software, on the other hand, what you see on the screen bears no direct relationship to what will appear on the paper in the printer. You don't even know where a page will break until you get a printout.

To some people, this doesn't matter at all. Their feeling is that thinking in terms of pages is a mere carryover from the old preelectronic days. In fact, they argue, one of the real advantages of word processing is that you learn to visualize a document as an entirety. Even if it goes on for twenty or thirty pages, thinking of it as a single unit enables you to shift material back and forth without hesitation, the end result being a better organized and more logical product.

The shifting around of words or paragraphs in the text is usually referred to as text manipulation, or text moves, in computerese. A group of words in the text is referred to as a block.

The basic text editing capabilities you want to look for in a word processor are block insert, block move, and block delete, functions that allow you to "cut and paste" by marking a block and then either throwing the whole thing out or using the cursor to deposit it in a new location. The so-called copy block—and one must bear with the jargon, for as yet there is no way even to ask what is available without knowing and using the jargon—allows you to make a copy of a block, yet leave it in its original place. This feature is handy for paragraphs used frequently in form letters and for boilerplate material to be inserted recurrently in reports, contracts, and the like.

Word processing software should also permit searches. A global search lets you find any given word in what is called a file, or document—that is, in the body of text you have produced. If you are writing a long essay on food and drink in the eighteenth century and you suddenly remember something you would like to add on the cisterns of Venice, you can type the word "Venice" into what computerese has dubbed global search, and the computer will then locate the place where "Venice" first occurs in the text. If that is not the particular reference you want, a push of the button will move the text on to the next occurrence of "Venice," and the next and the next, until you find the one you had in mind.

The capability to search and replace is an extension of the simple search function that enables a computer to find, say, every "Henry" in a file and replace it automatically with something else, say "Barbara." And now you see how all the

110

personalized junk mail that makes its way into your mailbox comes to have your name on it.

The search and replace function can also be used as a form of personal shorthand. Rather than typing out "word processing" thirty times in a file, you can simply type a *W* and, when you are all done, instruct your computer to replace each *W* with the whole phrase.

Another versatile feature that any good word processing program should have is the ability to automatically convert text into ASCII code. ASCII is the acronym for American Standard Code for Information Interchange, the computer world's equivalent of Esperanto. Translation into ASCII allows you to transfer a portion or the entirety of a document to another program that likewise deals in ASCII. It is also what permits you to transmit your prose over the telephone lines to another computer.

ASCII capability is not a visible feature, in the sense that you will not see it on screen, as you do, say, justified right-hand margins. Another invisible feature of some word processing packages is the ability to handle documents larger than the computer's memory by transferring the excess text to disks. But then, one must ask, how long does it take the computer to jump from internal memory to disk and back to its own memory again as it alternately reads and works on the document?

Does the program incorporate automatic reformatting? That is to say, if you make changes in the setup of a word-processed "manuscript," will the computer automatically make all the necessary subsequent changes in format for you?

What about page width? Will you be producing material that will always fit on a standard typewriter sheet or might you sometimes need extra-wide printouts, requiring a line width of 100 or even 200 characters? The provision for such a layout is a feature designed primarily for those who need to incorporate spreadsheets in their word-processed documents.

If spreadsheets are your bailiwick, then you will certainly want to be able to move individual columns of numbers, something that relatively few word processors permit. Then there is the matter of footnoting ability, again not one of the most common features to be found in a word processor, but an obvious necessity for scholars. Don't forget, either, to explore those more obvious but easily shrugged-off functions, mentioned earlier, such as capitalization, wraparound, and erase and unerase routines. Their relative speed and ease of use may make a large difference in your long-term word processing comfort.

These are but some of the more basic questions to ask as you begin your search for the word processor made for you. More questions will probably occur to you in the course of your quest.

Try out at least half a dozen different software/hardware combinations to see which best meets your specific needs and which is the most comfortable for you. If you love AppleWriter but hate Apple's keyboard, you won't be comfortable with them. Yet AppleWriter won't run on any other machine. Mouse compatibility is very important to some people, irrelevant to others. So don't forget to pet a mouse, while testing the various word processing packages, to see how it feels. But, above all, as you look, keep in mind the old techie saying, "It should be simple to do simple things and at least possible to do the complex." That's if, I might add, you think you might need to face doing the complex.

There are adjuncts to plain word processors. There are spelling checkers and proofreaders and outliners and more. You might want to weigh the advantages of a word processing program compatible with certain of these specialized programs. The Sensible Speller, from Sensible Software, CorrectStar, from MicroPro, and The Word Plus, from Oasis Systems, are a few examples of such accessory programs that cannot be used with all word processors yet can be very useful.

The Word Plus not only checks the spelling of words, but automatically hyphenates them, though not necessarily consistently with the style used by a particular publication. It also marks homonyms and counts how many times each word appears in a particular piece, a service designed to help in avoiding a repetitive vocabulary.

Carrying its copy editing even further, another Oasis Systems program called Punctuation and Style is designed to catch errors in punctuation and typographical inaccuracies such as repeated words and missing capitals. It also queries instances of mixed upper- and lowercase like THat—which gives writers on computer topics, who must cope with manufacturers insistent upon coyly naming their products Word-Star, VisiCalc, and so on, no end of trouble.

Part of the program is devoted to style. It lists phrases commonly misused and those that are "awkward, erroneous, folksy, muddy, pompous, redundant, or wordy." Personally, I refuse to let either word processing or its adjuncts infringe on my writing to that extent. However, I do find a spelling checker very useful for scrutinizing the final draft of a manuscript.

Since I use PFS:Write for text editing, the most natural choice in proofreaders for me is the companion package PFS:Proof, a program that can also be used with any word processing text filed in ASCII. PFS:Proof is a particularly interesting program in that it strives for a touch of artificial intelligence, or AI. As you use the program, it saves the patterns of your most common errors so that it becomes better and faster at ferreting out probable mistakes. Overall, the program is supposed to check a manuscript at the rate of 9,000 words a minute, which is fast compared to other proofreading software on the market.

The first time I used PFS:Proof, it stopped at my name heading the page. What puzzled it was not the first name, Erik—which surprised me, because this is the minor Scandinavian spelling and I had not expected it to be in the 100,000-word vocabulary of the PFS:Proof dictionary—but rather the first half of my surname, Sandberg. Highlighting the word, it offered no guesses. Since the spelling was correct, I requested the program to scan on. Getting as far as Diment, it suggested that the proper spelling might be "Dim net." Oh well, at least that was better than the salutation on a piece of computerized junk mail I once received. It had been addressed to E. Sandbugdammit.

Not wishing the spelling checker to repeat its verbal kickball with my name every time I ran a manuscript through it, I entered my full name and address in the dictionary. One is allowed to add 6,000 words of one's own choosing to the lexicon, which is a very handy provision for those dealing with specialized topics or involved in specialty fields. Most spelling checkers do not include, for example, brand names, such as Tandy or Compaq, designations used frequently by observers of the computer scene.

As to Tandy, the program guessed I might mean "Andy." After assuring it that such was not the case, I added Tandy to the dictionary. The TRS acronym often seen following on the heels of a Tandy reference produced a whole slew of guesses. "Ours," suggested the checker, then "tars, try," and suddenly "reds."

"It will try anything," Susan remarked in surprise.

"Roughs, rots . . ."

"Golly, I wonder how long this goes on."

"Out, to, st . . ."

"What's 'st'? Enough!"

"Tree, trace . . ."

"This is silly."

I had to agree. We went on to the next word.

A really great way to add words much used in some specific area of interest but seldom seen elsewhere, and thus absent from the dictionary, is to have the computer do the work for you. This feat is achieved by means of an option specifically directing the software to scan a completed file and add to its dictionary any new words found there.

You can call up your personal dictionary, the words you have added to the program's vocabulary, on screen. So if by chance it becomes full, you can go through it and delete some of the terms hardly ever used. However, you canot view the contents of the main dictionary. It wouldn't be the same on screen as it is in bound form anyhow. But not being able to know what's there bothers me. Perhaps I'm too much of a bibliophile. I enjoy scanning dictionaries every now and then.

More novel than spelling checkers and proofreaders, or even the grammar and form checkers beginning to appear on the word processing scene, are the software packages pre-

114

suming to broach matters of organization and style in writing. One such program is ThinkTank, from Living Videotext. Billed as "the first idea processor," the software is seen by its designers as "a visual tool for working with ideas and information"—which is another way of saying that it is an electronic outliner and organizer.

The program is easier to master than all but the most simple of word processors, whose software it is meant to supplement, not replace. A tutorial disk whisks you right past the manual, making you feel as if you have been running the program for weeks, even if this is only your second or third session with a computer. It takes you methodically through the organizational process of outlining, guiding you each step of the way, something which no word processor does.

Suppose you want to raise capital for a new business, a fast-food Swedish pancake restaurant, let's say, and you are working on the proposal. You wish to impress the hoped-for future backers of your pancake restaurant venture with its potential, and so you decide first of all to pull together as many relevant sources of supporting information on such an enterprise as you can. Sorting and alphabetizing these, you end up with twenty-three references indicating what a great idea it is. You save them under the heading Sources.

Next, you go on to describe the pancake idea itself, making Product Concept your caption and typing away, here and there inserting appropriate subheads such as Name, Uniqueness of Product, Consumer Benefits, Potential Frequency of Use, and so on. When you are done, you "collapse" this portion of the outline. What the computer actually does in this case is to remove all your text from the screen, replacing it with the simple Product Concept heading you have chosen to identify the section.

A careful culling of your sources focuses the market in your mind, so you enter your ideas on this subject under the caption Prospective Market. Collapse all the information in this category, and the screen is cleared for you to proceed to an analysis of the competition, your marketing plan, and financial projections, each given its own section. At that point, you ask for a printout and head for a well-deserved coffee break.

115

But now suppose that, while dunking a doughnut and clearing your mind, you come across an article in *The Wall Street Journal* on the drawing power of ethnic motifs in the restaurant business. The item would make a telling addition to your proposal.

So when you get back to the keyboard, you call up the heading Sources from your outline, "expand" it, calling the full text into view on screen, and insert the new reference. Then perhaps you decide to add the idea to your discussion of the product and to your marketing plan as well. You call up these categories in turn, expand them, and add a few selling lines to each.

However, as you are rereading the section on product concept, it begins to bother you. It's not as clear and direct as it should be. Something's missing.

You look at the subcategories in the outline. Of course! Variety, that's what's missing. Here you are planning to serve pancakes with twenty-six different fillings and sauces, and you haven't added anything about the impact of such multiple choice on repeat business. So you insert the subhead Varieties in both the product section and the marketing section.

The more you work with the outline structure, the more your concept grows. All you need to keep the screen hopping with ideas is the simple ThinkTank command menu that reappears at the bottom of the screen whenever you need it, responding with alacrity to a touch of the slash key. Nineteen basic moves allow you to jump back and forth, restructuring and adding to your outline.

In a sense, it's like being able to crumple up a piece of paper with your scribbled notes on it, throw it away and start over, and then, ten minutes later, fish the original idea out of the wastepaper basket and display it in its pristine form again. In another sense, it's like using file cards to outline your ideas, except that you don't have to staple two cards together when you run out of space, and you don't have to retype a card when you want to add something in the middle. Finally, you can have a summary of the outline printed up automatically whenever you want one. Frankly, I can't think of any better analogies than these, since ThinkTank is the first program of its kind.

Equally frankly, I'm not quite sure what to do with the program. A number of people I know swear it's the greatest thing they have ever seen for organizing free association thinking into a coherent, usable form. Personally, I found it attractive because of its ease of use and because of its serviceability as an introduction to computing for the ambivalent. But when all is said and done, I myself would never use ThinkTank for what it was designed to do.

Maybe I'm simply too disorganized to use such a program, or maybe I'm so visually oriented that I need to see physical scribblings in front of me on my yellow pads before I can feel that I have brought order to my thoughts. Whatever the case, I certainly don't like collapsing them to some nebulous world behind the screen where I have to shuffle them electronically instead of physically. Besides, there's a great deal to be said for the pleasures of crumpling up a poorly penned page and propelling it with rather more force than necessary in the general direction of the wastepaper basket.

Beyond the embodiment of our thoughts in word processing and electronified outlining, the personal computer, it seems to me, is bringing yet another, more physical change to the written word. A scribelike mentality is evolving among software publishers. Programs for producing illuminated manuscripts, twentieth century style, are filtering into the marketplace.

These programs, borrowing their theme from the decorative arts, enable a dot matrix printer, working in conjunction with a personal computer, to crank out all our deathless prose in a variety of font styles and sizes. But they tend to encompass a much broader visual scope than does the mere written word, containing as they do the ability to add illustrative material either of one's own design or from a catalog of electronic clip art. They are intended to offer the individual, through his personal computer, the artifacts of a home print shop.

The most basic of these type-enhancing programs has chosen that very image as its title, in fact. The Print Shop, from Broderbund, is billed as a software package that "automatically designs and prints greeting cards, stationery, and banners." The company should have added posters to the list.

The first thing my kids did with the program was to make up a fancy announcement with an ornately lettered Used Western Saddle For Sale caption to pin up on the bulletin board at the General Store.

The print-by-number picture portion of the program comes with a limited collection of sixty canned illustrations, including a cartoon zoo inhabited by a cat, a dog, a rabbit, and a penguin, among others, along with more specialized, symbolic animals such as a peace dove and a stork whose bill is laden with the once traditional baby-filled nappy. The inclusion of the Apple logo in this package designed for Apple II computers, however, surely carries boosterism a bit far. And there's no horse or unicorn, which presents a problem when selling a saddle.

Such a situation is not irremediable, of course. There is a graphics editor that allows one either to modify the existing drawings in the package or to add one's own computer-drawn artistic endeavors. For practiced game aficionados, the use of a joystick for this task probably comes naturally. For the rest of us, the fact that a KoalaPad can be used instead makes life a lot easier.

The KoalaPad, available for numerous personal computers from Koala Technologies, is a small graphics tablet that allows you to "draw" with a hard stylus on a small digitizing pad each pressure point of which, when touched, is sensed by the computer. To erase errors, you simply draw over them while holding down a button on the pad. You see on your monitor what you are drawing on the pad. When you are satisfied with the results, your picture can be added electronically to a poster or whatever else you are designing in your computerized print shop.

Because the Apple IIs have limited graphics capabilities, the drawings turned out with the aid of these machines have those jagged curves by now so familiar to most of us who have viewed computer art, rather than the smooth lines that even a three-year-old child can produce with plain crayons and paper.

All in all, I am still not sold on the wonders of junior da Vinci drawing by computer. Traditional media, even finger paints on the wall, offer far greater variety and far more opportunities for truly creative expression. Still, for the sheer novelty of it or for results intended to look exactly as if they had been achieved on a computer, The Print Shop is quite satisfactory.

The software's selection of fonts is limited. There are only eight typefaces from which to choose. However, they do offer considerable contrast, running a small gamut from Alexia, reminiscent of the Victorian Age, to a semicursive RSVP, Tech, which is techy, and Stencil.

Only two font sizes, large and small, are available. However, to lend more variety and an impression of further distinctions in magnitude, you can choose to have the letters printed three-dimensionally or in outline as well as in normal fashion.

Nine border designs provide for the framing of pictures or messages in design-them-yourself greeting cards, which seem to be the program's main objective. Additionally, a "tiled" feature allows you to create graphics patterns by taking a single design and repeating it, as if you were laying down a series of tiles, over a designated area.

Some rather clever printed letterheads can be created with the software, though it is not something one would want to do in quantity. The actual printing is a slow process indeed, because of all the dots the matrix printer must deposit on the paper in order to print those fancy fonts.

The whole affair reminds me of a computerized version of a little type case of rubber picture stamps and letters I had as a child. The set cost me all of $1.49, gave me hours of pleasure, and even resulted in some printed letters to an otherwise missive-deprived grandmother. In high school, I went on to hand-set real lead type and then ran off the results on classy bond paper. This more advanced kind of typesetting, with its concomitant greater variety, is represented electronically by the program Fontrix, from Data Transforms.

Fontrix offers an essentially unlimited number of typefaces with which to enliven the printed word. It also offers an interesting graphics design feature called a virtual graphics workspace, which permits you to expand your artistic endeavors beyond the limited screen. The screen before you is part of a larger picture whose contents are stored in the computer's memory. It's virtually like having a piece of paper five or six times the size of your monitor's picture window on which to draw. In the Apple version of the program, the extended screens can number as many as 16, in the IBM version as many as 23—or 115 if your machine is equipped with a hard disk. It is quite possible to create a banner a foot and a half wide and ten feet long, all in one piece, provided you have a printer capable of handling that paper width.

A feature more to the point for most users is the typeface editor's character cell, the work area for designing a letter in a new face. The cell measures a generous forty-eight by forty-eight pixels. Normally, software to be used in conjunction with dot matrix printers uses from six to ten dots in the vertical row and seven or so in the horizontal one.

The more dots there are, the blacker the type appears, although the jagged edges of curved areas are never eliminated entirely as long as a dot matrix printer is used. Fontrix is the only software I have seen that provides for enough dots to print really solid black type. It can even print negative type, that is, a solid black background with the letters in dropout white.

A magnify option enlarges the working surface of the character cell when the editor is being used in creating a new typeface, so you can shape the fine curves and points of a letter dot by dot. Completed letters can then be moved into place in copy or saved for future use by means of either the keyboard or an obedient mouse. Copy and overlay commands speed up the design process, for once you have created, say, a capital *P*, you can copy it and then simply add an appropriate stem to create an *R*. Any number of typefaces of your design can be added to your permanent collection of fonts.

Even if you are not about to assail the intriguing world of type designing, you can expand your store of available fonts by means of very reasonably priced Fontpacks. Each Fontpack contains ten separate character sets. Fontpack One, for example, includes in its collection a group of astrological signs, a selection of fancy borders, and eight different alphanumeric fonts. Fontpack Two, which describes itself as an art and technical package, provides electronic, mathematical, architectural, musical, and flowchart symbols as well as the Greek alphabet, since that language is much written, if less frequently spoken, in technical circles. Fontpack Four, billed as a foreign language collection, contains Arabic, Cyrillic, Hebrew, katakana, and Sanskrit, among others. And here is where the software's limitations begin to show.

At present, Hebrew and Arabic cannot be written right to left, nor katakana from top to bottom, so you must position the characters of these fonts individually, in the manner of laying out a mosaic. Future versions of the program should permit these typefaces to be set more readily in their normal fashion if the software is to be practical for typesetting anything more than short phrases or headlines.

Another drawback of the software becomes apparent when one tries to input text from an ASCII file. While I use PFS:Write for on-screen editing, I always make an ASCII copy of my *Times* column so that the story can be sent by modem over the telephone to the computer down at the *Times*. Thus, in theory, I should have been able to induce the Fontrix program, reading from my ASCII files, to print out one of my columns in, say, for variety, a Huxley Vertical font. However, my inducements were somehow not as effective as I could have wished. The characters were right, the line breaks were not. Ragged margins prevailed both right and left.

A call to Fontrix elicited the response that some word processing packages use a "soft carriage" return, which can cause problems. I had to line up the left-hand margin manually, line by line. Again it is to be hoped that this is an idiosyncrasy to be eliminated in the next version of the program.

As software goes, Fontrix is fairly time-consuming to conquer and a little less than "user friendly." When you receive an error message, half the time you are given no chance to correct your all-too-human mistake, but are instead returned posthaste to the menu, without much in the way of explanation. Still, Fontrix is basically a very useful package for those in need of special characters and camera-ready printed copy. For its relatively low price, it is the most versatile program of its kind that I have seen.

. . .

So there you have them, all the components of a marvelous new age of literature. You have a machine that makes writing the epitome of simplicity and efficiency, once you conquer the software. You have programs to check your spelling and punctuation, and ones that attempt to do the same for grammatical errors and fuzzy thinking. Finally, you have the means to print out the results of your literary endeavors in a fashion that would make medieval monks tearful with envy. Surely a renaissance of the written word cannot help but follow.

All the same, perhaps now is the time to stop and put matters in perspective. Is word processing truly the verbal Wunderkind it seems, or might it, just possibly, turn out to be no more than an exercise in verbose verbiage?

There is no denying that even a limited word processing program makes the writing life easier than a typewriter ever did. Add a spelling and grammar checker as a functional adjunct, even if it is less elegant and less effective than the idea behind it might have led one to suspect—one does, after all, still have to know something—and word processing becomes potentially a writer's dream.

Thus it was that the software came to trace its popularity to the members of the writing and journalistic professions, who greet anything that promises to ease their labors with joy. And if the elders of those vocations looked upon the new technology with scorn and trepidation, its almost instantaneous acceptance by the forward-looking of the tribes very soon established it as a standard occupational tool. It was only natural that, being writers, they should extoll its virtues in flowing prose. Initially, at least, as much was being written about word processors as on word processors.

But then a curious thing began to happen, not so very long after the pen or the typewriter was discarded for the computer keyboard. Much of what was being written became unintelligible.

One need not look far from the word processor itself to find examples of this lack of clarity. Take the literature of software and hardware documentation, for instance. The very use of the word *documentation* instead of *instructions* is heavy with obfuscation, however unintended. The literature itself requires translation into English before one can read it, unless one happens to be a microelectronics savant well versed in programming.

Over the last couple of years, I have heard word processing much discussed among writers and editors. My information has not been gleaned in any formal, interviewing sense. The topic crops up as naturally over a few beers as do Rupert Murdoch's latest moves. Interestingly enough, as in the Australian's mushrooming empire, the underlying trends in word processing portend a style of writing different from the styles of the past—less grand, though not necessarily less grandiose, more simplistic, even, perhaps, downright sloppy.

Until rather recently, writing implied a certain permanence. While the physical act of alteration became easier over the centuries spanning the transition from quill pens and parchment to typewriters and rag paper, it still entailed some labor. One tended to think before letting the ink flow.

Scribed electronically, words are ethereal forms. They appear, disappear, and reappear ephemerally, called forth by a Ouija board at the writer's fingertips. In such circumstances, the inscriber's thinking takes a new and different turn. The slow, deliberate, linear progression of structured logic, formerly used even when one was writing emotionally, gives way to a here-now, gone-in-a-second manner of composition. One's sense of continuity gives way to free-form thought. Dots of ideas resembling the dots making up the letters on the video screen drift in and out of one's consciousness, perchance to be captured, perchance to slip away unrecorded.

A lot of writers will rejoin that this is exactly the kind of freedom which makes word processing so useful. One can sit down and virtually pour ideas into the computer via the keyboard. Then it's so easy to change them, to revise them, to restructure the sentences, to move paragraphs, to organize and reorganize the thoughts that flowed so spontaneously.

Interestingly enough, the very ease with which changes

can be made often leads to their never being made at all. One tends to overlook a necessary revision in one's haste to capture a fleeting thought. After all, one can always go back and insert a "fix." But, in the end, it is forgotten. A manuscript looks so perfect in an electronic environment, where never a crossed-out word or insertion mark roams.

Individual sentences, too, look different on screen than they do on paper. They are looser, more fluent, more visually attractive. Overly long, Germanic sentences appear shorter on an eighty-character screen line than they do in print. So do paragraphs. Sometimes, carefully reading a printout of what seemed a perfectly good piece of writing on screen is akin to looking at something one wrote ten years ago. Well, maybe it's not so bad—but, really, how could one have settled for that?

Scrolling is as different from flipping through a stack of manuscript pages as watching television is from reading a book. You cannot put two completed pages next to each other and read them together when you are working with screen copy. Hopping around in a long manuscript becomes a kind of video jambalaya, where a feel for the actual words is, of necessity, almost totally absent. Connotative meaning gives way to denotative excess. Of course, if you want to change a character's name from Jane to Zelda throughout the manuscript, search and replace will do that for you automatically.

Add to all these unconventionalities the typographic pyrotechnics made available by such programs as Fontrix and the Macintosh's own MacWrite, which permit you to request your printout in any number of font styles and sizes, and the words themselves, in McLuhan fashion, may well become the message.

Word processing is undeniably useful. For some people, it is an aid to leaping over writing blocks; for most, a reasonably painless way to handle revisions. In businesses using form letters, it is becoming almost indispensable. Yet I wonder how much we are losing, on the whole, as we gain.

No doubt the same question was raised when the typewriter was new, and even when papyrus first became an annoying novelty to Mesopotamian clay tablet inscribers. Still,

I have the impression we are heading toward a future filled with the emperor's new words, where word processing cranks out fast-food prose, becoming to writing what xerography has become to the office memo: a generator of millions of copies of contentless phrases assembled for appearance's sake—rarely read, much less reflected upon.

8: Everything's Computing Up Crazy

The essence of the computer is that it is a general-purpose machine. This is what sets it apart functionally from, say, a toaster, which is designed for the single-minded purpose of toasting bread—oh, all right, in our progressive world, pop-up tarts and English muffins as well, but they are subsets of toast, so to speak.

Because the computer is a general-purpose machine, it can do whatever you want it to do. All that is needed is the software appropriate to the task, and you too will have power and control. The computer will be your slave. Thus, for years, went the salesman's spiel. To the consumer's question "What can I do with it?" he answered, "You can have it turn on the lights and the television and monitor the house for burglars and organize your shopping lists and index your record collection and catalog your stamps." It was the sense of power and control that created the myth of the home computer.

126

For the engineers, hobbyists, and others directly involved in the evolution of the machine, personal computing had always been a matter of power and control. The pioneering souls who spent $400 and hundreds of hours in 1975 and 1976 assembling the kit for that first personal computer, the Altair, were rewarded with a mechanism that could, with ten minutes of coaxing and having its front panel switches flipped, add two and two, delivering an answer of four. Of course, the red blinking panel lights that displayed the answer did so in octal, and since octal was a number system based on eight rather than ten, you had to convert the sum mentally into the numerical terms of our decimal system. The process was not unlike counting by the spaces between your fingers and then converting the answer into numbers based upon counting on the fingers themselves. It was also just a little slower. But the engineers were thrilled, and the reason they gave for their elation was power.

Now I must admit that I have never been all that power oriented. Pressing the keys on a calculator to determine that 32 times 43 equals 1,376 does not send a thrill of strength and control coursing through my fingers. Neither does running a spreadsheet program on my computer. Just because the machine ostensibly does what I tell it to do, I don't feel any great sense of control. Neither, I suspect, do most people. It is this that sets us apart from the hackers and true-blue computer buffs in our approach to computing.

Nevertheless, we had bought calc programs. We had bought word processors. Having seen microcomputer shipments leap upward following the introduction of the calc programs and then reach skyward with word processing, manufacturers were ready to scale the largest market of them all, the American home. All doubts were gone. Mr. and Mrs. America and their now somewhat reduced nuclear family were ready to embrace the marvelous future of personal computing. More importantly, so were the big, respectable corporations.

Texas Instruments, for instance, had a nice little computer, the TI 99/4A, available for a price roughly equal to that of one Walkman, one color television plus a portable black and white for the beach, a nice stereo, and a tape deck for the car, along with a food processor and an automatic popcorn machine. Surely every family was going to love having such a wonderful machine. Of course, the recurrent cost of intermittently adding software (had there been much to speak of, which there wasn't for the TI), would equal half of the family's weekly food budget. Still, how could the American family resist, wondered the industry.

How could it not?

While Texas Instruments was burying itself under half a billion dollars in losses, give or take ten million here and there, Commodore International, an old-line typewriter repair company originally from Brooklyn, New York, was busy selling the public on its computer. Commodore was successful, very successful, in fact, simply because it managed to manufacture its computers so cheaply that the selling price could be kept within the parental guilt range. "Doesn't your child deserve a future? What future is there for him in this day and age if you don't buy him an encyclopedia set—oops, I mean a computer?"

But Commodore, unlike Texas Instruments, had developed a fair amount of promising software for its machine, even though it promised far more than it delivered. Apple Computers had software too. Besides wooing the hobbyist and, increasingly, the small business markets, Apple had also begun to expand into the home. So at least there were some razor blades available to go with the razor itself if you bought one.

The final blessing was bestowed on the home computer industry by IBM when it brought out its PCjr in 1983. There had been so much prerelease publicity about this machine, code-named the Peanut, that the term "personal computer" was on everyone's lips. Even the local dog stylist was thinking of getting one. Ask him what he planned to do with it, however, and he was still stumped.

The best summation of the home computer market that I have ever heard came from an anonymous engineer once employed by Atari. Following its explosive growth in the video game marketplace, this firm had attempted to expand its horizons by making a couple of rather good home computers. Note that I said making, not selling.

The engineer in question was standing, somewhat befuddled, in the company parking lot, where he unexpectedly found himself together with the contents of his desk. Like most of the other employees of the suddenly almost bankrupt company, he had just been laid off.

"We built such a great machine," he said. "We thought everybody would want one. Turns out they'd rather go to the beach."

The promise of technology has always been convenience and comfort. From the central heating and air conditioning regulating the minienvironment of our homes to the food processor tearlessly slicing our onions, the fruits of engineering imagination that have succeeded in penetrating our daily existence have always had at their core the ability to make our lives easier.

The telephone more or less killed letter writing as part of our culture. It did so because it offered genuine convenience, not to mention eliminating worries over spelling and grammar. Even family word processing is not going to bring back correspondence as a personal activity, unless the breakup of AT&T leads eventually to a total breakdown of the telephone system.

If home computing is to be anything more than a passing fad, it will have to absorb something of the "Who could live without it?" quality of the telephone. Thus, high on the early list of what the computer could do for you were contributions to the culinary arts. Personal computing would invade the kitchen, armed with electronic cookbooks, automated grocery lists, and diet monitors. The expectation was that it would take over everything short of the actual cooking.

A lot of soon-to-be computer owners still have that culinary vision, minus the comic relief these kitchen programs have in fact provided. Out of the fifteen programs in the home applications category of the Softsel Hot List, two are cookbook programs. So someone must be buying them. The question is, how many buyers are using them? More to the point, how many are using them six months after they buy them?

I was reflecting on this dubiety during one of those "The cupboard is bare, I'm hungry, and I don't know what I want to eat" moments that somehow seem to strike writers at about four o'clock in the morning when they are halfway through a rush book assignment. Then I remembered the Micro Cookbook, by Virtual Combinatics (why does the mind call it up as Victual Combinations?).

I had been repressing the idea of running this program for quite some time. Since I have never even gotten around to filling out the index cards sitting unused and waiting next to the cookbooks, I found the prospect of my entering recipes into the computer an unlikely one.

Still, the Micro Cookbook promised a lot on its cover, from adjusting recipes to yield variable numbers of servings, to nutritional, caloric, and inventory control guidelines. On the subject of stocking the larder, it delivered a fillip of particular interest to hosts residing in the hinterlands like me or prone to entertaining company after grocers' hours.

"Tell your computer what ingredients you have," the cover instructed, "and Micro Cookbook will give you all the recipes you need to surprise your favorite guests." It would be interesting to see if the computer could solve my predawn predicament.

There are two disks to the Micro Cookbook. First the program disk is fed to the computer. Once that has been ingested, the recipe disk is inserted into the disk drive.

The Micro Cookbook is menu driven, which seems appropriate enough. The main menu presented me with quite an array of alternatives. I could be shown the recipe index, an ingredients index, a breakdown of recipes into categories such as French, dessert, meatless, and so on. Submenus could be called up to show actual recipes on the screen, to interpret terminology, and even to print out, provided I had a printer, a shopping list for any given recipe.

After experimenting for a while with the various alternatives, none of which I found enthralling enough to distract me from my original goal, I returned to the fillip that had attracted my attention in the first place, the one about how to find something interesting to concoct from the particular ingredients on hand. I entered my choice, SELECT FROM INGREDIENT LIST.

The screen lit up with a catalog of ingredients ranging from stew beef to cheddar cheese. Between these two listings, with less organization than that to be found in our Fibber McGee kitchen pantry itself, were white sauce, cognac, pignoli, Bisquick, kasha, white raisins, tortillas, and some 150 other items. Matching what I had on hand with the screen representations, I selected cumin, horseradish, and sausage and sat back to see what the computer could cook up.

The word *sausage* didn't quite fit into the space allowed. But since it was short only the *e*, and since in many programs of this type the software is designed to work with the first half or the first two-thirds of the word, I didn't give the problem much thought. However, in this case it didn't work, or maybe the program found the combination of sausage with cumin and horseradish not to its taste. In any event, I was greeted by a rude raspberry emanating from the program. "Serious error. . . . Terminating!" And terminate it did. Just like that, everything stopped dead in its tracks and the computer shut down.

The error messages section of the manual would admit to nothing so impolite as terminating. There was nothing for it but to reload both the program and the recipe disk. Meanwhile, I was becoming really hungry.

I entered only the cumin this time, to be on the safe side. "Swiss Cheese Salad Red Sauce," responded the computer, while the video screen asked me to type in which recipe I desired. The intriguing, if mysterious, Swiss Cheese Salad Red Sauce appeared to be my only choice. However, not wanting to take any chances, before entering my selection, I checked the icebox to be sure that there was some Swiss cheese around. I did not want to be hit with another termination.

As it turned out, all I could type into the allotted line this time was SWISS CHEESE SALAD RED. You guessed it. When I pressed the return key to actually enter the command into the computer, the program terminated once more. It became apparent that Swiss Cheese Salad and Red Sauce were two different courses, not served the one over the other, though there was no way to tell that from the display.

As I reinserted the disks yet another time, I viewed with

now gnawing hunger the missing bite in the Apple logo on the disk drive. Stifling my impulse to take a matching bite out of the disk, I worked my way back to pretermination on the screen, ending up with a recipe for Swiss Cheese Salad. Surprisingly enough, it even used horseradish—and sour cream. There was no sour cream in our refrigerator.

Dawn was breaking. I went out for a walk to alleviate my irritation. Returning by way of the chicken coop, I brought back a clutch of eggs, sat down at the computer, typed in EGG, and was greeted with a list of close to fifty recipes using "egg." Zabaglione didn't seem quite right at the hour. Potato salad was out. I never did like eggs in mine. I selected Eggs Florentine.

The recipe was simple enough. It called for "4 egg, 3 tbl butter, 2 tbl chopped onion, 1/2 lb cooked spinach." No spinach in the house. I shut off the computer, stared at the eggs for a few minutes, and then, deciding that plain fried eggs simply did not satisfy the "I don't know what I want" craving that had launched this entire endeavor, put them in the icebox. As an afterthought, I put the disks in the freezer. I went to bed with an inspired thought: the Micro Cookbook really was the American Dream, a guaranteed-to-lose-weight diet plan.

A newer version of the program is slightly easier to use and has some of the glitches removed. Still, who needs it? Or who needs an even less fulfilling program like A>Cook, from East Hampton Industries, designed exclusively to organize and computerize one's recipes? For that matter, whatever is a computer doing in the kitchen anyway, a greasy environment that is surely one of the worst possible for a machine of that nature?

I like to cook. I also like to thumb through cookbooks and boxes of recipe clippings. The cookbooks do have indexes. As to clippings, why should I spend weeks and weeks cataloging and entering them into a computer when I could be cooking and eating instead?

• • •

Of the thirteen best-selling home applications programs on the Softsel Hot List besides the two cookbooks, nine are word processors and four are money management packages. Now word processing promises writers, business people, and students certain attractive features, and the students may live at home. Otherwise I can see no connection between the activity and the abode. Money, on the other hand, is, like food, something few of us can live without, which might help to explain how money management programs ended up on the Hot List. Whether they also end up on the use list instead of the closet shelf remains to be seen.

There are numerous budgeting programs, tax preparation programs, and checkbook programs on the market. What separates Andrew Tobias's Managing Your Money, on the MECA label, from the competition, besides the well-known personality backing it up, is that it puts all the pieces together. Actually, it does more than put them together. To use the current buzzword, the software is integrated. In other words, its various program functions interact.

Let's say that you sit down once a week for about half an hour, as the program suggests, to pay your bills. Then let's say that, instead of writing out the checks yourself, you enter the pertinent data into the computer and have it print out the checks for you.

That would not be a great timesaver, you point out. True enough, it wouldn't be. In fact, it would probably take you slightly longer to pay your bills that way than it would using the traditional pen and checkbook, which is why the check-writing programs currently available are not really worth very much.

However, in the case of Managing Your Money, the information you enter transfers itself automatically to the other sections of the program. For instance, let's say you have it make out a check for $125 to the dentist. Besides printing the check for you, the software enters the amount as a deductible expense in the income tax section of the program, deducts $125 from your net worth, and matches the amount against your budget.

At the end of the year, provided you have really kept up with your data entry, your taxes have already been largely calculated for you. Meanwhile, you have a continuous update of your financial position.

The portfolio manager, which handles the investment side of your affairs, is quite sophisticated. Not only does it automatically enter the results of your transactions on your tax form and sort them into ordinary and long-term gains and losses, but it makes pie charts, also automatically, of those investment results as well.

The question is, do you really need pie charts showing your profitable trades and unprofitable losses in percentages or dividing your income into wedges used for evenings out, interest payments, and so on? Probably not. One problem with Managing Your Money is that it complicates itself with more features than most people want.

Another problem is that while the program is, overall, reasonably easy to use, it is not quite as easy as the publisher and Tobias would have us believe. For example, although the IBM PC has a numeric keypad like those found on calculators, Managing Your Money, for technical reasons, will not let you use this keypad to enter numbers. Instead, you must use the number keys located at the top of the typewriter keyboard. For anyone who deals with numbers on a regular basis, this is a real inconvenience.

Using the space bar to move on to the next screen in some segments of the program and the F1 key in others is another inelegant solution to a programming problem that should not have been particularly vexing. It is a small point, but one conducive to distraction and annoyance.

More serious is the omission in the tax section of schedule SE for the self-employed and schedule F for farm income. The two groups of people needing those schedules are the ones that could probably put the full power of Managing Your Money to better use than most of the rest of the population.

Then there's the decision to minimize the size of the instruction manual. Ostensibly this decision was made because "nothing is as deadly as a computer manual." To that I would like to add "except, perhaps, having to read video screen after video screen of material that would have been better put in a book instead."

The screen verbosity takes on a rather smart-alecky tone at times as well. No one, and especially not the neophyte, needs comments like the one in response to a request for help too early in the game, which reads, "Are you checking to see whether the help screen has changed? Well, it has, but there's still nothing to say." Even with copious on-screen verbiage, furthermore, the instructions fail to direct the user adequately in spots.

For example, one is not warned that if one holds down the F9 key to go back a number of pages at a time, the computer may lock up. I saw someone panic when this happened, as the computer kept reading the disk over and over again. He knew enough not to turn the machine off, since doing that could ruin the disk drive as well as the disk. But he didn't know how to stop it.

The solution to a dilemma like this, which holds for most software, incidentally, is a "soft boot," consisting, for the majority of computers, of pressing the control, alternate, and delete keys all at the same time. This combination will take the computer back to square one. You will have to start all over again by loading the program. But that's better than ruining the drive.

In tune with the big-name-personality hype of Managing Your Money, the publisher, glossing over the hardware facts, lists the minimum equipment needed to run the program as being a computer with 128K of memory and one double-sided-disk drive. Only after you have purchased the package and begun to use it do you realize that a color monitor is needed for the graphs and that, if you do not have two disk drives, the switching back and forth between the three software disks is going to resemble an afternoon of shuffling cards.

Basically, Managing Your Money may be a useful package, and even, at times, an instructive one. For example, I reduced my use of seat belts from 100 percent of the time to 0 percent in the life insurance section and duly watched my life expectancy drop and my insurance requirements increase in response. But it still lacks much of the convenience that could make the program a must-have, except perhaps for people who actually enjoy living the game of Monopoly on a day-to-day basis.

The other home financial packages available today are, for the most part, even more frustrating and irrelevant to the average individual's monetary resources than Managing Your Money. There is a little of value in all of them, but usually not enough to justify spending either the time or the money they involve.

At a recent Future Computing seminar on home computers, Scott Cook, president of Intuit, which publishes a check-writing program for microcomputers called Quicken, asked the audience of personal computer executives, "How many of you use software for your home finances?"

Eight out of the 180 present raised their hands—and I'm willing to bet seven of those did so only to make him feel better. The fact is that an estimated 99 percent of the financial software designed for home use remains unused. Packaging and hype sell the sizzle. The contents turn out to be wasted time and frustration.

• • •

Speaking of frustration, one of those visions belied by the facts is that of the pastoral life. My family and I learned this rather early, quite soon after our return from a citified existence to country living. Because we have the land, which I would hate to see go to ruin, and because we enjoy its harvests and a rural existence, we keep the soil tilled and the barnyard filled. But farming, even on a small and homesteading scale, can confound the would-be farmer to an extent never hinted at in the bucolic scenes so often depicted in association with it. Take shepherding, for instance.

Contrary to popular folklore, counting sheep is not something that puts you to sleep. It is an endeavor much more likely to to result in tense frustration.

Sheep tend to look alike, and even if you are on a first name basis with them, telling one from another can be difficult. Thus sheep breeders install tags in the ears of members of their flock. The sheep, in turn, remove the ear tags with the aid of fences, brush, or any other handy protrusion.

To solve these and similar problems, certain manufacturers are beginning to make ear tags, mostly for dairy cows but

136

applicable to sheep or other livestock, designed to be implanted under the skin, where they will not be subject to the wearer's removal. The question one might well ask, however, is, how does the farmer read them?

The answer, as I am sure you have guessed, is that he doesn't. His computer does. Each ear tag is self-powered and sends out a tiny coded signal. The signal indicates to the computer which passing animal is wearing the tag, and the machine indicates in turn how much the cow or other creature should be fed, when it should be bred, what its milk or other desired production is, and so on. Meanwhile, as it goes about its monitoring duties, the computer is also building up a data base. It's all eminently practical, as many data bases are—if they can be dealt with.

But what exactly is a data base? And how come software companies seem to feel that every home should have one, whether there happen to be sheep or cows out back or not?

In point of fact, our day-to-day lives are filled with data bases. Chances are you've never looked at life that way. Then again, you're not a computer. But take the telephone book or, for that matter, the ubiquitous grocery list flapping from its magnetic anchor on the refrigerator door, enter it into a computer, and suddenly it's a data base. So, housed electronically, is your address book, the library's card catalog, and that shoebox full of expense records and canceled checks stuck back in the closet after the agony of April 15th. With the rise of the personal computer, the term "data base" has become almost commonplace. Yet the phenomenon itself is still somewhat frightening to many people. It need not be.

What separates a data base from plain information is simply organization. The computer is not a necessary part of it, except perhaps by connotation. Consider the telephone directory again. There are computerized versions of it for the use of the telephone company. The book itself is computer typeset. But the physical, coffee-stained, scribble-covered volume is as much a data base as its electronic counterpart is, albeit not as flexible a one.

Look at the entry "Allen Aardvark, 33 Banana Lane, 555-0111" in a telephone book. In data base-ese, such an entry is

137

known as a record. If a mini-telephone book had eight separate listings, the data base would be said to contain eight records.

Now if you were to draw an imaginary vertical line between the names and the addresses of those eight records and another between the addresses and the telephone numbers, you would have further classified the data, or information, into fields, each containing similar information. The first column, listing all the names, would be one field, the column of addresses would be a second field, the numbers would be a third. It all seems a bit like reinventing the wheel, or in this case the telephone book.

So why do it? If you want to turn your family address book into a computerized data base, frankly, I can't think of a single reason to support your whim. For a small business, on the other hand, as for a large farm and like enterprises, a personal computer data base could well be an important tool.

Let's say you found the number 555-0111 scribbled on a piece of paper marked "Return call. Urgent." Such a situation would be unlikely to arise at home. The note would be more apt to say "Dad, call your boss back right away" or "Genevieve, call Rachel. Urgent." If it did give a number, you would probably recognize it as a familiar one, if not one you could immediately place. In a business situation, on the other hand, with only a telephone book at your disposal, you would be unable to determine whom you were supposed to call. But a properly set up data base enables you to look up any record, provided you can can determine the content of one field. So given the number, 555-0111, the data base could give you the name, Allen Aardvark.

Consider another example, a little more complex but still simple enough for our purposes, namely, a pet store with several hundred regular customers. Let's say the owner is very promotion minded, so he has his staff note the specific details of every purchase over $10. In addition to the three or four fields mentioned, he makes room for ten more fields on each record—the owner, the date of the sale, the name of the pet, and so on. At the end of each month, by having the computer sift through the various fields, the store owner can call up the names of all the people whose dogs should have been groomed and weren't, or send personalized computer letters to all the tropical fish fanciers, announcing a special sale, or, as a service, mail a vaccination reminder to all the people who bought cats a year ago.

Please understand that here I am not by any means advocating computerized salesmanship. I am simply giving you a sampling of how it works and, by inference, an idea of one direction in which the so-called personal computer revolution is taking us.

While most computer data bases are essentially not much more complex in nature than the one in the foregoing example, making use of the information they contain may be something else again. It is often far easier to put information into a data base than to get it out.

In some data bases, for example, the fields are too short to contain their rightful contents without abridging them. What happens to poor Allen Aardvark if the main field is limited to ten characters? At best he becomes Allen Aard, at worst an insulted ex-customer.

Another common failing of data bases is that the files are too inclusive. Our pet store owner may enter the date of grooming and the name of the pet into one field instead of two. A year later he decides he wants to send birthday cards to every dog he has sold, but he can't separate the pooches' names from the shampoo due dates.

Neither of these problems, nor the countless others to be encountered in delving into data bases, are irresolvable. But the time to solve problems is before they occur. So if you have occasion to set up a data base of your own, think through its potential uses carefully before you start filling boxes. The effective utilization of a data base depends on a well-planned and orderly arrangement of its parts. Fail in foresight and you will pay in frustration.

While the appropriate potential uses of a data base, in my opinion, do not include any for the home—neither filing recipes nor generating shopping lists nor cataloging one's records nor any of the other applications foreseen by computer enthusiasts as being indispensable—business uses are some-

139

thing else again, and even a small home venture may profit from a computerized data base.

A cottage enterprise as modest as raising a small flock of sheep, for instance, might be made more manageable by having a personal computer do the paperwork for it. Such, at least, was my thought as I reflected on data bases and their lesser applications. Electronic ear tags and the like accoutrements of large-scale agricultural computerization were not for us. But a neat little file on our sheep, everything in one place safely inside the computer, might well be.

Because a portable computer could be lugged right out to the barn, and since the outbuildings were equipped with electricity, I decided to use the Commodore SX-64, reposing idle and unused at the moment in the computer room, for our experimental on-disk sheep records. Had I wished to carry a computer out to the fields along with my shepherd's crook— yes, I have one, what is a flock of sheep without a crook?—I would have had to use a lap computer, something like Radio Shack's Model 100 or Hewlett-Packard's 110. The SX-64 is portable in the sense of being lightweight, tipping the scales at nine pounds, and possessing a convenient carrying handle. But though it includes a tiny monitor, it has no built-in power supply, so you are tied to the umbilical cord of a power line.

Sitting in my office, I set up a working data base framework for our forty sheep, creating what seemed likely to be the relevant fields: registration number, flock number (to be changed if the ear tag had been lost), name, birthdate, pedigree, inoculation record, lambing history, wool yield, and so on. Then I entered all the data already on hand for each sheep, information previously kept on physical file cards instead of electronic ones.

It was the medical records that were my primary interest in computerizing the files, however. Knowing when, for example, the worming boluses were last administered and the enterotoxemia and tetanus injections last given is essential to maintaining a healthy flock. Yet normally these crucial dates and doses were noted on scraps of paper in the barn, which had a way of becoming very elusive indeed.

When one spends the day wrestling forty sheep, one is

prone to be less than tidy towards the end of one's tour of duty. Even when the paperwork is successfully completed, it tends to be trampled underfoot in the chaos, if it is not altogether blown away in a gust of wind when the barn doors are opened at last to let the flock loose again. Overall, the day's report had always acquired a somewhat indecipherable appearance by the time I got it back to the office for entry in the official records, a task most likely not tackled with any urgency.

The computerized data base would solve all these problems at once if I could simply enter each bit of new information as it developed. Thus it was that the Commodore found itself on a grain cart in our barn.

Worming sheep is simplicity itself—in theory. You grab a hind and a fore leg on the far side, flip the animal over, and set it on its rump. A sheep so positioned is almost completely immobilized and does not struggle. The other thirty-nine, however, are all over the place.

With the first sheep cradled between my knees, I pronounced its ear tag to be number 239. Susan called up the appropriate file on the Commodore's screen, Tanya loaded up the bolus gun with thiabendazole, Genevieve went to round up the next sheep, and Revell went chasing after a chicken not in the mood to be petted. Then Susan duly entered date, dose, and a notation that the left side of this particular ewe's udder had acquired a small laceration while she was out to pasture. I applied spray iodine and urged my wife and my computer to hurry up and finish their entries before my back broke.

So it went, one sheep, several additions to the data base, next sheep, several entries, and so on. As usual, each sheep seemed to be heavier than the last, even though I had started with Mixup, our new 350-pound stud ram. But that's not the sort of data one enters.

When we were finally done, Susan and I collapsed onto hay bales. "I'm not sure how much time this saved us," Susan remarked.

"Neither am I," I agreed. "But at least the information will all be there for a change."

My words were no sooner spoken than I spotted Oscar, the world's meanest rooster, up on the grain cart where the computer rested. With the unfailing accuracy of his bare instincts, he had started pecking at the floppy disk. By the time I almost had my hands around his neck, he had bitten the bytes. Scratch the new data base.

Somehow, uncomputerized farming, at least on our diminutive scale, suddenly seemed much the easier of the alternatives open to us.

The rest of that particular day did not offer much by way of consolation for our lost sheep records. As I discovered on returning to the study, the water line had broken somewhere along the 600 feet between the spring house and my office. My trusty old steed, Tiny Ticket, who thinks he's still young enough to jump Volkswagens, had by evening developed a renewed case of the heaves that had plagued him in recent months, a particularly bad bout that made me wonder if he would soon be a candidate for Tufts' student autopsy team. I remembered that my tax bill, deferred by extension, was now unalterably due, something no tax planning program could help me with. And by dinnertime a computer company had called with an offer to fly me to Japan for a few weeks to view their new products, a proposal that for obvious reasons of business propriety I could not accept, no matter how much I love sushi. It was enough to send one off the deep end with TENSION!!!

Then, lo and behold, as I was finally opening the day's mail over my after-dinner coffee, I came across a black box with a picture of fleecy clouds scudding tranquilly across a blue sky. On it, in bold script, was printed *Relax.*

Was someone trying to tell me something? No. Well, perhaps. It was another piece of software to check out for review. Considering my condition, the bills due, and all the day's setbacks, my natural instinct was to collapse into bed. But my next week's column was due the following evening, and newspaper deadlines are stern taskmasters. The software so opportune in its arrival at least seemed appropriate to review at the moment. I trudged over to the computer room to have a look at it.

142

Relax turned out to be "The Stress Reduction System," from Synapse Software. It came complete with a seventeen-page *Getting Started* manual to elucidate the running of its software disk, a headband, an electromyograph (EMG) unit, and a stress-reducing audio cassette.

Since I had an IBM PCjr still set up from a recent review, I selected the disk containing the version of the software appropriate for that machine and loaded the program according to the instructions. The screen lit up with the Relax logo, displayed in wandering stripes of colors, as some most unrelaxing sci-fi beep-beep "music" beset my ears.

Still following the instructions, I wrapped the headband around my occiput and forehead, plugged in the EMG unit, and turned it on. Nothing happened.

The next line of the directions told me to check the batteries. Flipping over the EMG unit, sure enough, I found a covered battery slot. My blood pressure rose. Now they told me!!! Here I was, strapped to the computer like some junior Frankenstein, and they wanted four pen cell batteries!!!

"Of course, I always carry around a pocketful," I muttered as I tore off the headband. The only batteries around were in the PCjr's keyboard. Cannibalizing these, I loaded up the EMG unit and switched computers and disks.

Calling forth the computing powers of a Commodore 64, I entered its customary clumsy command, LOAD"*",8,1., another great example of home computing "user friendliness." While I waited for the disk drive to run at its usual snaillike pace, I put on the headband and turned on the EMG box, which now emitted the comforting red glow of a power light.

The Relax logo eventually appearing on screen was followed by a main menu listing four choices: Main Menu (F1), Kaleidoscope (F5), Graph (F3), and Game (F7). The solipsistic inclusion of Main Menu on the main menu at first seemed rather strange. But because the program is so simple to operate and requires so few selections, I suppose this is to remind you that, no matter where you are in the program, simply pressing F1 will immediately return you to the menu.

Graph, my first selection, turned out to be composed of a

500-point vertical scale plotted against a horizontal elapsed-time line. It also proved to be the real centerpiece of the program.

The scale is a relative one. The numbers have no absolute meaning, the states they measure have no "normal" reference point. They indicate merely how relaxed you are at one given moment as compared with your condition at the previous moment.

There are eight different per-second sampling rates. In the version of the software designed for the Atari and the Apple, they range from 60 to .25 seconds between readings. For other computers, the range is from 30 to .25 seconds.

In addition to varying the measurement rate, you can select either the jagged representation of a direct, real-time sample or the mathematically-smoothed-out graph of an average sample. I found the latter mode the least visually distracting—once I got my tension on screen.

My first attempt to have the computer visualize my aggrieved mental state indicated that the headband was failing to sense my angst. To test it, I was supposed to clench my teeth and watch the tracing line on the graph shoot up. It didn't, even when I bit into an old walnut.

The manual suggested checking for hair trapped between the skin and the sensors on the band. In my case that was obviously not the problem. My hairline is receding sufficiently to offer about an acre's worth of bare forehead for the sensors to have located themselves on.

The next suggestion was to swab the sensing units with a saline solution or a gel in order to improve contact. Great!!! I had salt but no water, and the nearest source of Vaseline was the diaper table at the house. Somehow the thought of once more unplugging myself from the computer and going all the way over there for a spoonful of petrified petroleum was aggravating enough to make beads of frustration form on my brow.

Voilà! Contact! The graph began tracing.

The EMG unit has two slide switches, range and fine tune, to set the point at which the trace begins graphing. Manipulating these to give me a starting point of 450, as instructed, I sat back to watch my taut nerves in action.

I must say, if the results of running Relax are indeed an accurate measure of tension, in my case those results were very interesting. For example, if I wrote along smoothly, sentence after sentence, and happened to look up, I often found that the trace had dropped 50 points while I was so engaged. From the blisters on my pen-holding fingers, I had always thought of cranking out articles and similar such prose as a rather tension-producing activity. On the other hand, a satisfying half-hour tea break spent reading in Richard Jefferies' *The Amateur Poacher* produced an even larger drop—which was as it should be.

My one regret was that the program did not have a print feature. Even with the trace set to record one measurement every four seconds, the first segment of my reading interlude had long since marched off screen by the time my tea was finished.

My anxiety having begun to abate, I decided it was time to try some of the program's other features. Selecting Kaleidoscope, I was met with the tones of what seemed to be an erratic electronic gamelan player and a series of, you guessed it, kaleidoscopic images whose changes in color and pattern were supposed to mirror my relaxation.

This was definitely California culture. An Easterner myself, to the point of having leanings toward the distant side of London, if not Vienna, I mumbled, mimicking President Reagan, "Aw shucks, there you go again," and switched over to The Balloon Game.

And I quote. "The balloon game lets you reap the benefits of your learning with the graph and kaleidoscope. In this challenging game, you control the flight of a balloon with your tension level. You must catch the bubbles that enter your screen from the right while avoiding the pins from the left. . . ." Alternately relaxing, to entice the balloon down, and clenching my teeth, forcing it to ascend, I played the game for ten minutes or so before realizing that I was about to give some orthodontist unexpected business.

Switching back to Graph, I tried some yoga deep-breathing exercises left over from a college days' fascination with Eastern cultures and watched with satisfaction as the trace drifted down 150 points. My success encouraged me to tackle the last item in the package, the audio cassette, whose contents are supposed to aid in one's relaxation training. Plopping it into my old Sony, I was greeted by a gibbering Donald Duck on speed. The machine's drive governor was obviously shot. The trace rose 200 points, and I decided it was time to call it quits for the evening.

Returning to the house around midnight, planning on regaining 150 points of relaxation in a hot bath, I let myself in the door just in time to hear that the water pump had gone on the fritz, probably from sucking air through the broken water line.

Do you know what would really sell me on the idea of there being a future for home computers? A digital plumber at my beck and call at two o'clock in the morning.

9: The Little Electric Schoolhouse

The mid-1980s will be noted in the annals of computer history as the point at which educational software became a recognized, in fact even a curricular, part of the childhood learning experience—and at the same time met its Waterloo. What brought about this peculiar dichotomy was the early hype surrounding home computers. If your child did not become "computer literate"—went the argument—there was no way in which he or she could ever progress beyond the status of clerk or waiter in the employment world of the future.

Guilt! It's a wonderful thing for selling parents almost anything.

Put guilt aside, however, and a totally different picture emerges. Certainly, the demand for people to fill high-tech jobs appears to be exploding at the moment. But that is only because there were so few high-tech jobs around a decade ago.

Base any comparison of this nature on initial figures low enough, and the increased opportunities will appear to be limitless, when in reality they are far from being so. No tree grows to the sky, and, according to the Bureau of Labor Statistics, the seemingly endless abundance of high-tech employment opportunities, so much in the lime-light today, will actually end up accounting for only 6 to 7 percent of the total number of new jobs created in the eighties.

That's jobs, please note, not computers. The machines themselves will be at almost every job location, just as tele-phones are now. But how many people, even though they use the telephone constantly in their day-to-day dealings, know, say, how packet switching works, or even, for that matter, what packet switching is?

People don't need to be "telephone literate" in order to benefit from this electronic instrument. The same holds true, or should, for computers.

Some children take naturally to learning computer lan-guages and writing software, just as others are adept at mas-tering biology, French, history, music, or baseball. Their skills are a combination of talent and interest, neither of which can be fostered by computers per se, no matter what the manufacturers may claim.

In point of fact, the overall quality of educational comput-ing right now is so awful that its effect on students can only be largely antithetical to the fostering of anything besides boredom and discouragement. There is little in the current software stamped "educational" to stimulate curiosity or evoke an intellectual interest.

Far too much presumptively instructive software, particu-larly for the younger set, is simply electronic page turning, at best enlivened with crude sound effects and cruder graphics. A child being "taught" by a computer reads something, most likely a question, on the screen; types in a response, most likely a number, if the material is structured in a multiple-choice format; and is rewarded, if his response is the correct one, with trumpet fanfare or some other laudatory signal. An inappropriate response is greeted by some token of displea-sure. Then a new screen is called up and a new question presented, and so on. Such software does not provide even the flexibility of a book.

One of the flaws of computerized learning often overlooked in the rush to promote educational software is that you can't take it with you. What a child can't tote along gathers dust.

Children, since time immemorial, I should suspect, have preferred to read, play games, and do almost everything else imaginable almost anywhere but where they are supposed to do those things. Give them a nice study desk, and they will spread their books and papers all over the living room floor, unless, of course, it's dinnertime, in which case their study materials will be scattered over the dinner table.

The computer does not lend itself to being hauled out to the kitchen table or propped up on the living room floor. It certainly does not feel comfortable in the steamy bathroom. You cannot readily brush crumbs off a keyboard, and a video monitor with milk spilt on it is capable of monitoring nothing at all.

On the computer's side of the literacy ledger is the oft cited, and presumed crucial, benefit of "interaction," which is a buzzword for the student doing something and the computer responding in some way. Interactive software, by supposedly giving the student a sense of control over the machine, and, hence, the learning process, allegedly causes the child to become so absorbed in the task at hand that he or she learns without even being aware that the acquisition of knowledge is taking place. However, having watched numerous children, including my own, become bored after half an hour's worth of one of these programs, I can't help but feel that they are, most of them, a waste of a child's time and a parent's money.

Unlike children, the computer never becomes bored. This attribute of the electronic personality is maximized by another prevalent type of educational software: drill and practice routines. Working with such programs, students need never fear their electronic tutor's impatience, while at the same time they need suffer no embarrassment over repeatedly giving the wrong answer until the correct one has been conquered.

Yet even here much of the software available is, frankly,

not worth its price. Why spend $30 or $40 on what is essentially a set of electronic flash cards, for example? Numerous beginning math programs put a pair of numbers on the screen and then ask students to add, subtract, multiply, or divide them. A $3 box of flashcards, particularly if the parents become involved in the contest, will do the job better and more easily. The kids won't even have to type in the answers.

Typing is, however, something that anyone dealing much with computers will have to master, and here the machines can truly be of help. I well remember a certain elderly blond Valkyrie of positively operatic proportions hovering around my shoulders while my fingers tripped over each other on the typewriter keys. "What all of you must realize," she said as I x-ed out a line in frustration, "is that this typing class is probably the most vital course in your whole high school curriculum."

Considering what few specifics I can recall from my high-school education and what fewer I use today, perhaps she was right, although none of us would have agreed with her then. In any case, that episode was what crossed my mind a few years ago when Genevieve sat down in front of the Apple II Plus to try out Typing Tutor II, from Microsoft.

At the time, Genevieve was in the sixth grade. She had expressed a desire to learn how to type, and considering that her last extensive contact with a typewriter had been the disassembly of an old Smith-Corona in third grade, perhaps it was indeed time for her to move on to more positive applications. The arrival of Typing Tutor II had been opportune.

Upon loading the program disk into the computer, Genevieve was faced with three headings, Fast, Lessons, and Slow, across the top of the screen. In the column beneath Lessons was a line of letters to be practiced. Beneath Slow appeared numerous lines of gibberish seeming to contain every symbol on the entire keyboard (which they in fact did, this being the first lesson). The column below Fast was vacant.

Even without looking at the manual, an omissive tradition in our family as in most, Genevieve soon deciphered the fact that her assignment was to copy exactly the text appearing in the Lessons column. The results of her efforts appeared directly below the line she was imitating, and letters she typed quickly and accurately enough would move from the Slow to the Fast column, indicating her progress.

As Genevieve was pecking away at the keys, I was reading the manual, which is, unfortunately and as usual, not as good as the software itself. Particularly noticeable is the inadequate description of the proper finger placement for touch-typing. The *ASDF* and *JKL;* keys are listed as being the constituents of the home row, to which the fingers should always return; but the keyboard illustration accompanying the first lesson does not in any way accentuate that home row for quick identification, as most typing manuals do. Even more importantly, the manual does not explain in any detail which other keys are to be activated by which fingers. Saying that "nonhome keys are typed by extending the appropriate typing finger" and then giving as an example only the reach from *D* to *E* for the middle finger of the left hand does not adequately cover the ambiguities for the self-teaching beginner.

Using Typing Tutor II in a school environment complete with an instructor/supervisor is a different story, naturally. The program can track the progress of as many as forty-nine students. It also permits a teacher to create customized tests. I would thus expect the classroom to become one of this electronic tutor's areas of greatest success. But it is still a handy, if not completely satisfactory, program for self-education.

Genevieve attacked the business of acquiring her typing skills with all the vigor she once imparted to playing Frogger, in the days before its novelty paled. After building up some speed with the eight-character practice lines, which cleverly use more and more new characters farther from the home row as a student's skills increase, she moved on to paragraphs.

The first paragraph to appear on the screen was full of nonsense words and arbitrary-looking groups of characters. Genevieve objected. "PDL? That's dumb."

Actually, of course, it wasn't dumb at all. The program's emphasis is on developing proficiency with the letters the would-be typist most needs to practice. Nevertheless, Genevieve was not alone in demonstrating that the nonsense does

151

tend to induce impatience on the part of the user. Susan, who types 100 words per minute but dislikes the feel of the Apple keyboard, somewhat reluctantly joined the family software-testing team. Whenever she came across a string of words particularly distasteful to her, she would say something like "Two 'jaffas,' I'm not going to do that one!" and hit the escape key, taking the program back to the menu where she could choose a new paragraph.

The escape feature is a convenience, but one readily over-used. Genevieve, for instance, striving for accuracy, would hit escape whenever she made a mistake, because the program seems to have no backspacing capabilities and thus no apparent means of correcting an error. The latter restriction, though traditional in the pedagogy of typing, seems a rather strange carryover to computing in view of the fact that clean copy is an explicit goal of word processing.

One of the strengths of Typing Tutor II, particularly for the achievement oriented, is the program's progress report, which breaks down the typing results by such categories as average number of words per minute, best words per minute performance, and average number of errors. The words per minute score, however, does not take errors into account. I managed to provide an extreme example of this discrete scoring by simply holding down a key to take advantage of the computer's repeat function and thus typing considerably above my normal speed. To be precise, I came in at 103 words a minute, according to the display. My accuracy on this same test was 3 percent. Personally, I think the traditional method of subtracting the number of errors from the number of words typed provides a better indicator of one's true typing ability.

The structure of the proficiency tests and the program's design to zero in on the typist's weak spots are very useful features of Typing Tutor II. The inability of the user to turn off the sound, on the other hand, is an annoying drawback. Not everyone wants to listen over and over again to fifty-nine successive beats as all the keyboard characters are listed under the Slow heading, and to all the other beats and grunts that emanate periodically from the computer.

Typing Tutor II has been on the Softsel Hot List of best

sellers for over two years now, and a new release, Typing Tutor III, distributed by Simon & Schuster, has recently joined the original on the Hot List. While I have not yet had the opportunity to try out the new Typing Tutor III, from what I have heard, its improvements include a much faster response time on the part of the computer, an on-screen help facility, and a remedying of many of the weaknesses of Typing Tutor II. Like its cohabitants on the Hot List, Type Attack, from Sirius, and MasterType, from Scarborough Systems, Typing Tutor III tries to interest children in "saving the universe" by shooting down attacking alphabets.

The stated objective is not quite as silly as it might appear to us older folk brought up in a pre-video-game world, and these programs appear to be quite effective in teaching a basic feel for the touch system. Certainly, younger children seem more attracted to this type of learning situation than to straightforward tutorials. But I have found one modification of the hardware, shall we say, to be imperative, and that's covering up the keyboard.

Somehow, in the enthusiasm of the game, the concentration of a child shifts rapidly from learning the layout of the keyboard to merely shooting down the unremitting battery of letters and words. It is not an intentional thing, but players almost inevitably look down at their fingers to make sure that they are in the right place at the start of the game. The next step is to look every time they press a key. Soon the entire game has become a series of hunt-and-peck attacks.

My solution to this problem was a cardboard box large enough to fit over the keyboard with the fingers in place and sturdy enough to stand alone with one side cut out so the hands could be freely inserted. One must bend down and peek in order to line the fingers up on the home row at the beginning of the game. But from there on all a player sees when absent-mindedly glancing down to make sure that the fingers are on the right keys is the enigmatic cardboard box.

If a task such as teaching the touch system seems a little mundane and down to earth for a computer, there are others more unexpected and out of the ordinary. One might even say that there are others more remarkable and, so to speak, out of this world.

• • •

It was a crisp fall evening, and a new moon was just peeking through the now bare lower branches of the linden tree in our front yard. Susan, Genevieve, Tanya, and I were all sprawled on the terrace looking skyward for shooting stars, while Revell was busy counting sheep, figuratively, not literally.

Pointing to a group of stars below and to the right of Cassiopeia, Genevieve queried, "What constellation is that, Dad?"

That's when I remembered TellStar II, from Scharf Software Systems. This stelliferous software package is designed to help one identify luminaries in the heavens above. Limited, understandably enough, to the identification of fewer than all the visible objects in the sky, it has other features to offer in compensation for this necessary shortcoming. For example, it can transport the viewer to any place in the world from which he or she chooses to observe the firmament. Though not for everyone, it can add considerably to the observational pleasures of those interested in astronomy.

Because of the numerous and complex mathematical calculations involved in the program, loading TellStar II takes some time. To be more precise, it takes almost six minutes on an Apple, two on the IBM PC, although if one's IBM is equipped with a math coprocessor, a special chip dedicated to number crunching, the software will load in just a few seconds. Even with the Apple version, however, the wait is worth it.

Once TellStar II is ready to run, one needs to define the point on earth from which the computer is to peer out at the sky. Not surprisingly, the location to which the software is initially tuned is Boulder, Colorado, home of Scharf Software. But by pressing the N key, for "new selection," when the location menu is displayed, you can enter the latitude and longitude for your own position. This location then becomes the software's new standard, called up automatically every time you run TellStar II. Of course, you can always switch places on earth—repeatedly, for that matter, in case, for instance, you wish to practice celestial navigation by sailing across the seas from Tahiti to Easter Island under the Southern Cross on the ship of your imagination.

TellStar II presents the sky both overhead, simulating the view straight up toward the zenith, and as a horizontal vista. At the side of the screen are displayed the date, the time, and, for those really involved in astronomy, the sidereal time, or local hour angle of the vernal equinox. (The sidereal day is about four minutes shorter than the solar day by which we run our affairs.) You don't have to know anything about sidereal time in order to use TellStar II as an observational guide to the heavens, but, if you are a meticulous amateur astronomer, this feature of the program is very handy.

The sidereal time for the solar date and time of the sky you wish to view is calculated automatically by the software. If your computer is possessed of a real-time clock, which is nothing more than the name implies, a clock in the computer that tells the machine what time it is in our world, TellStar II will gather this data by itself. Otherwise you will have to enter the solar date and time manually. The computer will do the rest.

The program, incidentally, is capable of displaying the sky as it appeared or as it would appear at any time from the year 1 to the year 3000. So there is no need to worry about the software becoming outdated. The greatest accuracy, however, according to the publisher, is for the years from 1980 to 2000. Progressively greater degrees of deviation can be expected as your astral time capsule strays from the present.

Speaking of accuracy, TellStar II will automatically factor in daylight saving time if you are not among those so bitten by the astronomy bug that they refuse to reset their timepieces according to governmental whims. The program's star tables are also adjusted automatically to compensate for precession, the slight wobble of the earth about its axis, caused by the gravitational pull of the sun and the moon.

One factor for which a complete adjustment cannot be made, however, is the discrepancy between the essential flatness of a video display and the spherical nature of the sky, the earth's surface, and, consequently, our view of space. Be-

155

cause of this insurmountable lack of accord, a certain amount of distortion is inevitable. Logically enough, the overhead view presented by TellStar II is more faithful to our perception of the heavens as seen by the naked eye than the horizontal display is.

Distortion becomes particularly noticeable when one presses the magical *C* key, putting the program into the constellation mode. Here is where the computer draws lines between the stars making up the visible constellations, from the familiar outlines of the Big Dipper to such relatively unknown silhouettes as Crater. In the horizontal display, the distortion of any of these groupings appearing in the upper elevations causes them to seem almost like new and unique constellations.

What the TellStar II constellation mode draws are the simple connect-the-dotted-stars images of modern celestial maps, not the ornate mythological figures of the ancient sky charts. Orion wears no bearskin and carries no gnarled club in TellStar II's heaven.

Still, the program does neatly locate and define the various constellations. Of perhaps greater interest is the fact that it locates almost anything else you might want to find in the sky as well, including 110 Messier Objects.

Charles Messier was a late-sixteenth-century comet hunter who used to spend his evenings on the roof of the Hotel de Cluny in the Latin Quarter of Paris. Unfortunately, he kept finding bright deep-sky objects which, when viewed through a small telescope, looked like possible comets but weren't. To help others finding themselves in his repeated plight, he cataloged these galaxies, open clusters, and nebulae as false leads to be ignored in future comet searches. Today his series makes an excellent first observation list for owners of small telescopes.

If you have a telescope with alti-azimuth locating circles, you can use TellStar II as an automatic locator for the Messier Objects and other heavenly bodies. Using the software's locate mode, you simply enter the name of the particular astral body you have decided to pursue from the tables at the back of the manual. The computer then either responds with the announcement "Object below horizon at this time" or, if the entity is visible, supplies you with its location as regards its right ascension, declination, elevation, compass heading, and so on, for setting your telescope's alti-azimuth circles, as well as the time it rose, when it will set, its magnitude, and, in the case of a planet, the phase it's in.

The identify mode, which is my own favorite, supplies the same details, but in this case you single out a particular object you wish to identify by sliding a small set of crosshairs around on the screen until they are on top of it. A small C appearing near your target will indicate that it is a constellation. If you aim at the C and press the space bar, you will discover immediately whether it is Cassiopeia or Lacerta. Home the crosshairs in on one of the small squares representing the Messier Objects, and the computer will determine whether that particular stellar entity is M46, the galactic cluster in Puppis, or M47, the open cluster in the same constellation.

If you have a printer connected to your machine, you can have a printout of any given night sky portrayed on the screen to use for notations or a log simply by pressing the print key. However, be sure that everything is in order and ready to run before you make such a request. The first time I asked for a printout, the printer was not plugged in. The computer gave me an "Out of paper" raspberry, the program shut down, and I had to start all over again.

It was annoying, though not fatal. Another mildly annoying feature of the program, or rather the manual, is the lack of an index. Then too, a computer printout is never as good as a regular star map from a planetarium or from one of the astronomy magazines. To reap the true benefits of TellStar II's celestial explorations, one needs the computer right out there beneath the starry sky.

At least that was my rationale as I headed back to the house on that crisp fall evening for a 200-foot extension cord and the machine itself. Susan came with me on my second trip to pick up the monitor and the software.

Our return was met with another query from Genevieve. "Mom, how have you put up with this guy all these years?"

Susan didn't answer. Then again, I suppose that's the kind of question one can't answer.

After connecting all the computer components in the chill

of the autumn night, I powered up and loaded the TellStar disk. My doubts over how the machine would operate in the somewhat frosty environment—I was particularly worried about the mechanical disk drives—were stilled as the program's logo jumped onto the screen.

Entering the appropriate date and time information, I requested an eastern sky display to coincide with Genevieve's unknown constellation. The horizontal viewing mode, however, was so distorted by the flat screen that we soon switched to the overhead mode. Since this covers the sky only from an elevation of forty degrees to the zenith, we had to wait a while before our stars hove into view on screen. At first the constellation was still too close to the horizon to be visible on the computer projection.

Three fairly bright shooting stars followed by what could have been a streaking nova, so brilliant a trail did it leave, made me feel that luck would be with us. The earth turned. Tellstar's map on the screen turned. Genevieve and Tanya, having gone back to the house for a couple of rugs to stretch out on and blankets for covers, were continuing their search for meteors with their eyes closed.

When the constellation finally made its way high enough to be identified, it turned out not to be one. Even determining this fact proved to be a rather difficult feat. The video monitor screen with its brightness reduced to the barest minimum was still too luminescent against the darkness of the evening, impairing our night vision. The star map, as clever as it had seemed indoors, and clever though it truly is in concept, was too distorted, even overhead, to match the actual sky. Too few dots rose on screen compared to the myriad of wonders punctuating the night. The screen was too small, the sky too large. Besides, I soon tired of holding the monitor above our heads. A paper star chart is much more easily sustained aloft.

The identifier mode remains a neat feature in my mind. It's still my favorite of the software's many aspects. But somehow, that night, for a moment I suddenly saw it for what it is, only the first crude step toward what will need to be a vastly refined system if it is to even begin to fulfill its promise. There was more excitement and thrill to be found, I think, in the

158

small three-and-a-half-inch reflecting telescope I scanned the skies with as a child.

Personal computers tend in general to remove the personal from experience. The chemistry sets and basement laboratories of my youth, the potassium permanganate crystals ready to turn water into "blood," the collected cocoons liable to release their secrets at any moment, the jars inhabited by grasshoppers, frogs, and snakes—all the packrat paraphernalia of childhood curiosity, in short, seems to have largely vanished, replaced increasingly by the ubiquitous personal computer and its electronic kin.

Scholastic is now even marketing Operation Frog. Billed as a "leap forward in science," this software package left me staggering in amazement at the potential chaos it could bring to education. Once in possession of Operation Frog, the budding young scientist will no longer need to cut up a preserved frog specimen in order to analyze its parts. Instead, he will disassemble its crude graphic representation on screen. That will be so much less messy, the company points out, and no one will have to overcome any squeamishness such dismemberment might induce.

But the program starts out with the usual cartoon frog catching a fly and then jumping off a lily pad to swim around, with just the eyeballs visible above the surface of the water. At one point the eyeballs each go their separate ways around a lily pad, no doubt producing a great deal of mirth the forty-fifth time a student runs through the program and has to wait and wait to get down to action. More importantly, the diagrammatic frog bears as much resemblance to the real thing as a sixteenth-century map of the Americas does to the actual continents.

The trend toward scientific examination once removed puts a barrier between the individual and a certain crucial contact with reality. Like it or not, manipulating a slithery frog in a dissection tray with probe and forceps is an experience very different from the one offered by its symbolic counterpart on screen, however vividly portrayed. It also presents a far greater range of possibilities, from its stomach contents to an unexpected muscle scar, than its computerized counterpart

159

could ever reasonably provide. And herein lies a question not to be lightly dismissed.

Will all this electronic wizardry create a generation out of touch with reality? Quite conceivably, it could produce a population possessed of only minimal hands-on experience of the real world. On the other hand, the recent fear of seeing our country's youth become totally immersed in video games dissolved with a peaking of interest in that fad. In like fashion, the devotion to computers per se as tools of analysis will hopefully give way to more broadly based and more encompassing concerns and activities.

A possible precursor of things to come is AtariLab, a software/hardware package developed at Dickinson College. AtariLab puts the computer in touch with the real world, albeit in a limited fashion. In doing so, it expands the machine's horizons—and those of its users.

AtariLab's basic starter set contains an interface, a special plug-in module that allows various sensors to be attached to the computer. Whatever these sensors detect, temperature or light, for instance, can then be fed directly into the computer for the machine to "feel" and deal with.

The set also includes a temperature sensor for the computer, in the form of an electronic thermometer, along with a regular thermometer for the experimenter, a 16K software program cartridge to run your projects, and the manual. A second AtariLab set, The Light Module, should be available by the time you read this book. Additional modules are planned.

The AtariLab experimenter is guided through the 150-page handbook of experiments by the AtariLab dragon, a friendly and inquisitive beast wearing the archetypical lab coat with pen-filled pockets. Starting with the basic requirements of experimentation and a general discussion of how a hypothesis is developed, the introduction covers the setup of a typical scientific inquiry. It does so without being rigid or dogmatic in tone, explaining that "scientists do not usually follow these steps exactly." This open-endedness and the encouragement given the student to question and expand on the experiments are nice attributes of the manual.

160

Typical of the AtariLab projects is the old kitchen chemistry experiment of mixing baking soda with vinegar to produce carbon dioxide. Here, however, the experiment is used to show the difference between exothermic, or heat-generating, and endothermic, or heat-absorbing, reactions. The instructions for the experiment are peppered with leading questions, such as "The foaming that happens when the carbon dioxide is released seems energetic. Where does this energy come from?" Various hypotheses of what is occurring follow.

Another experiment you can carry out involves measuring the dew point so regularly mentioned in broadcast weather forecasts and exploring the concepts behind it. You can also determine the response time of the electronic thermometer, discover the most efficient way to cool a liquid such as soda, and learn why water containing salt is so difficult to freeze.

The software accompanying the temperature module not only enables the operator to measure the changing temperature of a reaction in either Celsius or Fahrenheit but to graph the results on screen over various time frames as well. Data can be recorded over the life of the experiment, and the interval between measurements is easily changed. With a printer, it is also possible to produce hard copy for use in a written report.

AtariLab's experiments are not suggested for children younger than fourth graders. However enthusiastically youngsters tackle the projects, and however basic and detailed those projects are, an adult assistant is helpful.

Getting started can be the most difficult part of the AtariLab venture for a young child. As Tanya pointed out when she was experimenting with the set, the on-screen instructions are not always complete. For example, the budding scientist may be instructed to proceed to a specific menu, such as Choose Time, but not be told how to do so. On the other hand, Tanya did figure out by herself how to proceed, in what has become youth's traditional failing-all-else approach to the computer: when in doubt, press some buttons until something happens.

Besides the many experiments offered, the AtariLab handbook includes appendices on calibrating the electronic thermometer, writing BASIC and LOGO programs for converting temperatures from Celsius to Fahrenheit, entering log functions, and creating files. There's quite enough to take the advanced junior scientist beyond the simple experiments into a whole world of tantalizing exploration.

So perhaps there is indeed reason to hope that realistically oriented software may materialize, at least in fields of endeavor where the computer can serve, not as unrestrained game master, but as efficient scorekeeper and loyal research assistant. All the same, I find it just the tiniest bit difficult to imagine anything on screen ever really being as satisfying as certain endeavors of my slightly misspent youth, such as building rockets and otherwise peering into the more explosive side of my basement laboratory.

• • •

If I were seriously to regret anything in that possibly somewhat misguided but blissfully exploratory early existence, it would be that I never managed to acquire any musical skills. In part, that was a genetic fault, for I am relatively tone deaf. I love to listen to music. But don't ask me to hum a few bars and expect anything besides auditory anguish in return. The other factor contributing to my nonmusicality was a certain lack of patience.

For the vast majority of people, probably, impatience is the single largest deterrent to conquering a musical instrument, either as youngsters or, more especially, as adults. Most of us simply haven't the endurance to start with "Twinkle, Twinkle, Little Star" and progress on up through the prerequisite scales toward musical proficiency. Besides, somehow it seems embarrassing to be playing such simple tunes as adults.

But enter MusiCalc 1, from Waveform. Part of a total musical system for the Commodore 64, this program turns that particular computer into an all-out music synthesizer. It also allows one to start playing quite complex compositions almost instantly.

The program achieves this goal with the aid of a little cheating, of course. How else could it possibly bypass those all-important ingredients of learning, patience, and practice? It provides a series of preprogrammed melodies with which one can play, arranging and rearranging sequences, adding sounds, harmonizing the results, experimenting with different rhythms and special effects. It puts the novice over the learning hurdle and right into the middle of the fun of music.

At the same time, it allows for an exploration of music that has not been possible heretofore, not easily, at any rate. So perhaps the tradeoff—instant immersion versus an omission of the fundamental elements of musical training—has a certain arguable validity. Then again, a true musician might protest that such play is neither constructive nor creative.

What no one with any musical interest or ability will dispute, however, is that MusiCalc has something for everyone, from the beginner to the accomplished performer or composer, who can use it with the same verve with which he or she attacks a full-scale music synthesizer costing thousands of dollars.

The program takes full advantage of the Commodore 64's special tone generator, a device far more versatile than that found in its place on any other personal computer today. Instead of producing merely the noise of bombs and crashes and bells and gongs, the cacophony associated with so many video games and even much of the so-called educational software, Commodore's Sound Interface Device, or SID, a three-voice generator, can originate a triad of distinct and different tones at the same time, say melody, bass, and percussion.

Speaking of percussion, ScoreWriter, the second disk in the MusiCalc series, includes software that permits you to connect various extra digital sound effect devices, such as drum machines, to your electronic orchestra. But the more basic function of this particular program, as it is used with MusiCalc 1, is to translate your compositions into standard musical notation and then print out the results complete with staves. Executed by a Commodore VIC graphics printer, these scores seem, at least to my musicologically uncritical eye, quite adequate, although the flags on notes sometimes appear to run together and the dots on dotted notes are not always distinct.

Effortlessly acquiring a printed score might be something

163

of interest primarily to the professional musician, but MusiCalc's save feature is something for everyone. It allows a player to record a composition on disk electronically for later replay or reworking.

Beyond the basic MusiCalc 1 and 2 lie templates present and planned offering further scores for the intrepid experimenter. Currently, two templates, African and Latin Rhythms and New Wave and Rock, are available to expand the repertoire of MusiCalc. More are on the way.

All these prerecorded snatches do not make using MusiCalc a completely effortless endeavor. Nor, unfortunately, does the poorly written manual make the would-be musician's life as easy as it should be, considering the capabilities of the program. However, conquering MusiCalc takes less patience than, say, correlating the upper-register notes from sheet music with the fingering on a clarinet.

With MusiCalc, there are no squeaks or off-key notes. What you mean to play is what you get. And if you don't like what you get, you can simply make some adjustments on the edit display, which is where you enter the sounds you want, one at a time, defining the notes and octaves, and then play it again. Switch to a different screen display showing a mockup of the type of music control panel you would find on a specialized synthesizer, and you can manipulate sliders, represented by zipperlike pictures, moving them up and down by means of the keyboard to raise or lower the volume of and otherwise shape a particular note, until everything sounds just right. Whatever you do, and however often you do it, the computer's patience once more has no limits.

MusiCalc will not turn anyone into a Mozart or even a Boy George, but, starting out by adding your own innovations to preprogrammed melodies, you can relatively easily, if slowly, go on to create entirely original compositions. The program is like a huge auditory Erector Set. You begin with the basic sounds and rhythms of music, then, composing on the keyboard, you build and rebuild on these until the software takes your composition to wherever your ear and mind have led it.

Probably the biggest problem with MusiCalc is the clumsiness with which a composition must be entered into the computer, by way of the on-screen music control panel. Another music program, Melodian, from the company of the same name, bypasses this obstacle by including a piano-style keyboard that plugs right into the Commodore. Although the inclusion of the keyboard makes this package a little more expensive than just buying the MusiCalc program, it is not much more so, and the additional cost is really more than made up for by the simplicity of operation.

When you use the Melodian keyboard, each note you play appears on the screen looking like a regular note. You can save that music on disk to play again, you can have it printed out on standard staves, you can manipulate the composition every which way, all using only four control keys. You can even mix multitrack music, starting out with, say, a bass track and then adding, one by one, guitar, brass, and woodwind.

You can also create new sounds, new instruments. The traditional instruments, as a matter of fact, have a rather new sound to them too. For example, the clarinet, although its tones are more mellifluous than my squeaky childhood renditions of "The Old Missouri Waltz," has an electronic mood about it, and does not rank with the real instrument well played.

My musical taste is admittedly old-fashioned, having only recently progressed to the point where I will intentionally listen to something as modern as the compositions of Leŏs Janáček. This leaves me in somewhat of a quandary when it comes to performing computers.

Over and over again, I have been besieged by prophets of the harmony of the electronic spheres, who have assured me that the realms of tonality are indeed the proper territory of computers, that these machines will open vast new auditory avenues for us all. Bachian fugues in particular seem to be subjected to the calculating counterpoint of computers. Thereby processed, they seem to me to emerge as soulless tympany.

Part of this effect is a natural result of the still relatively primitive state of the art of computerized music as a whole. The effect is not helped any by the fact that the instrument used to achieve it is a personal computer with a sound chip so poor that even "Old MacDonald" played on it turns an honest-to-goodness barnyard into a symphonic setting by comparison. Yet the computer's performance is greeted by enthusiasts with ohs and ahs of delight. One cannot help but compare the reaction of computerists in such an instance to that of parents marveling at a baby's first "Goo-goo."

There is more to question here than the simple sound effects. Are computers, for all the mathematical parallels to music, suitable instruments for composition and musical expression?

Outside the influence of that ponderable question, however, lies a separate area, where the computer is not used as a synthesizer, but rather as an adjunct to music theory instruction. In this quieter place of learning, it may well make its most valid musical mark.

One such teaching program is Apple Music Theory, from the Minnesota Educational Computing Consortium. Another is Musicomp, from Apple itself. Not feeling myself adequate to the task of testing the pedagogic qualities of these software packages, I enlisted the aid of Dr. Catherine Wade, our children's music teacher. Endowed with several decades of practice helping youngsters of all ages in their struggle through the learning curve of musical appreciation, she had expressed curiosity about the potential role of computers in music education.

Musicomp turned out to be, frankly, a disappointment, in large measure due to its dependence on the Apple's sound-generating capability, which is akin in tonality to a rooster gagging on rosin. The program plays music from a repertoire of twenty-four selections, ranging from preludes and romances to gavottes, minuets, and fugues, and displays the executed notes on the screen. Select, say, the ever popular "Jesu, Joy of Man's Desiring," and one is greeted with agonizing tones as the music proceeds inexorably to its end, the notes composing its score marching disconcertingly from right to left across the staff on screen.

The first two chapters of the manual go into such basics as range, key, and time signatures, voice, and timbre. The third chapter, on making music, begins, "If you have skipped straight to this section . . . ," which shows a degree of foresight on the part of the author, since that is exactly where everyone I have seen try this program begins. The third chapter is where you find the meat and potatoes and indigestion.

The program assumes that you know a fair amount about music. To begin with, since there is no instrument-like keyboard or on-screen music control panel to use, the program requires that you either know how to read music beforehand or, as the manual puts it, "find a friend to help you."

But, as Dr. Wade commented, "If you have to find a friend to learn how to read music, it would be easier to use a recorder," meaning the simple, nonelectronic wooden instrument from centuries ago.

One already familiar with musical notation, on the other hand, soon discovers that while the program does allow you to enter and modify new music, as opposed to merely playing with prerecorded melodies, it does not permit you to write harmony.

Too advanced for the novice, too elementary for the professional, the software falls into a musical no man's land. The computer as tutor loses again.

On the positive side of the educational ledger, Apple Music Theory is a real find for serious music students. It's not that the Apple's tonal quality suddenly improves, but rather that for this program it simply doesn't matter much, and the software utilizes to advantage that unique quality of the computer known as unlimited patience.

Music Theory covers a broad range of subjects from aural to visual intervals. It includes lessons on key signatures, note types, enharmonics, counting, rhythm, and rhythm play, as well as scales and exercises in excising wrong notes. The sections on musical terminology are of less merit than some of the others. Terms, after all, can readily be acquired by reading. But the drill and practice sessions, devoted to such endeavors as the identification of intervals, triads, chords, and the like—anything to do with training the ear, in short—are valuable and well done.

The teaching style of Music Theory is one of presenting the student with a set of queries on a given subject. For aural intervals, say, you can specify the intervals to be drilled, whether the notes are to be presented from high to low or vice versa or as a mixture, and the number of problems desired. If you enter, for example, OCTAVE, the computer plays an interval for you to identify, you enter your answer, and the computer responds with either "No, the answer was . . ." or, hopefully, "Correct, the answer was . . . ." In either case, the correct answer is supplied, and the computer keeps score on how you are doing and where your weaknesses lie.

Dr. Wade's summation, after evaluating the two programs, was, "To me, this is much more exciting. Of all the subjects in music school, this was the one I had the most trouble with. To be able to work like this in a nonthreatening environment is super."

• • •

The academic environment has certain menacing aspects from which there simply is no escape short of withdrawal. One of these is the competitive edge being put on the student's learning situation. We are in many ways becoming a nation of numbers rather than persons, and information seekers rather than knowledge gatherers.

Perhaps nowhere are these trends better exemplified than in the current emphasis on testing. Scholastic tests, aptitude tests, psychological tests, job-matching tests—they all rank people numerically, with the apparent precision of inviolate integers churned out by computer scorekeepers. Occasionally a hue and cry is raised about the tunnel vision these examinations are fostering. But, on the whole, society seems to have decreed that, in a thoroughly modern, high-technology world such as ours, delineated by computers, binary judgment is the only logical, productive way to mark man among his fellow men.

Now the examiners are taking a giant step, direction not specified, in defining the nature of future testing. No longer is the computer to remain relegated to the mundane position of scorekeeper. Rather, it is to become the actual tester. The software for this task will be designed to inspect and scrutinize the individual weaknesses and strengths of the test applicant and modify the examination to accommodate that person's personality and skills—even as he or she is being interrogated. The resulting inquiry will be quite similar, in fact, to an interview.

Fortunately, or at least not surprisingly, the test taker is being equipped to take up arms against the test maker. His armor bearer is a personal computer, his sword a program, one of the increasing number of software packages addressing themselves to the academic grail of the eighties.

The earliest target of these cram-by-computer testing tutors was the College Board examinations, soon to be joined on the target map, I have no doubt, by a full range of boards—law, medical, veterinary, and what have you.

One publisher of electronic SAT tutorials is Krell Software, which offers a money-back guarantee for its College Board SAT Preparation Series. Not about to retake the SAT exams myself after all these years, I had no way to check out the effectiveness of these programs. However, Krell warranties at least an 80-point improvement on a student's test score after using this software.

Computer SAT, from Harcourt Brace Jovanovich, is also designed to help the student achieve a high score on the Scholastic Aptitude Test. The software provides test-taking exercises in the three distinct areas of mathematical, verbal, and vocabulary skills, prefaced by a series of practice tests to help you develop a personal study plan. The questions for these tests are in a book. Only the answer blanks appear on the computer screen, which becomes your self-scoring answer sheet.

As in the real world, Computer SAT allows questions to be answered out of sequence, as I discovered when I clutched over the antonym of *effulgent.* It also allows you to change your mind. If the answer you have given for, say, question 12 suddenly seems wrong, you can type 12 O, for "omit," and then type in the correct answer. Of course, it would have been more convenient to be able to strike over the mistake with the new entry without having to "erase" it first.

Another convenience would be a more detailed explanation in the user's manual of what to do next when you have done something wrong. While trying to get one of my practice tests scored, I made an incorrect entry and suddenly found myself looking first at a blank screen, then at the unfathomable statements, presented in succession, "Open test control . . . Read test control . . . ? Re-enter."

I felt as if the teacher had rapped me across the knuckles with a ruler.

Quickly I typed YES, MENU, STOP, NEXT. Not one of those was the magic word, apparently. I resorted to that old computer standby, Control C, also to no avail. Admitting defeat, I turned off the computer and restarted the program, fully expecting to find that I had lost my test results. It was a pleasant surprise to find my answers still intact on disk.

Unlike the practice tests, the Computer SAT drills allow for direct entry of the answers to the questions, which are displayed on the screen one at a time. For some math questions, the computer will ask if an explanation of the answers is wanted. It does not seem interested in elucidating other questions.

Once you have become familiar with the routines, it is relatively easy to jump about among the drills and computerized flashcards in search of the areas of inquiry most in need of work. The computer couldn't care less how often you romp through the same file.

One real drawback of the program's mode of operation is that where there are, say, forty test questions, their numbers are presented in four columns, with room for the answers to ten of them in each column. Yet if you want to enter answer B for question 16, you must type 16 at the bottom of the screen, followed by a B. The computer will move your B to the 16 on the "answer sheet." It would be much simpler, and closer to a real test situation, to be able to enter your B right next to the number 16 already on the screen.

A mouse could remedy the situation. Assisted by this nimble electronic rodent, you would need only to slide the cursor into position and then press one of the mouse's ears once for A, twice for B, and so on. Mouse-assisted testing software will probably be available within a couple of years, if not sooner. Given their own way, manufacturers will speedily make the mice as much a part of modern life as computers themselves.

170

10: A Mouse around the House

The computer-conscious mouse first scurried across my path at the Las Vegas Convention Center in the fall of 1982. The computer trade fair Comdex was in full swing, and the booths crammed into the convention hall were teeming with new products and fresh salesmen. Personal computing had come a long way in half a decade and a bit.

Casting an eye over the exhibits, I reached the conclusion that the marketeers of personal computing had run through most of the familiar fruits in search of people-comforting nomenclature—apples, oranges, limes, and peaches had already been appropriated to sell Apple hardware, Peachtext software, Lime surge protectors, and the like—and were now setting their sights on the zoological world. Witness, for example, Leading Edge's Elephant floppy disks. However, the biggest computer news personality of all at the time was the pachyderm's mythological archenemy, the mouse.

There were mice all over the Convention Center, not among the neon-flashing, balloon-frosted displays of new computers, disk drives, and tantalizing graphics systems, but scuttling about beneath the tables and in hidden boxes backstage of the booths. With so many firms trying to be both first to the cheese and secretive to the end, the marketing strategy in evidence appeared to parallel the psychology of *Mus musculus* itself.

Mice as data entry devices actually first entered the world of computers as long ago as 1967, when Douglas Engelbart fathered the first potentiometer-driven rodent. Eventually taking the form of a soap-bar-sized box with a couple of buttons for ears and a long tail connecting it to the computer, this device measured changes in electrical potential through belly wheels as it was pushed back and forth across a hard surface. Using analog, rather than digital, technology, the mouse's movements were translated into computer-intelligible information and used to guide a pointer on the computer's monitor screen. Cursor direction could thus be controlled without the operator having to use the keyboard.

While that might not seem much of an accomplishment, a mouse coupled to the right software makes accessible a whole new style of computing. Instead of having to deal with Cartesian coordinates, striking the cursor keys, say, seventeen times for left and twelve for up, one can reach a desired location on the screen simply by moving the mouse so that the cursor slides directly into the appropriate division, traveling with ease even diagonally.

Essentially, mice allow a nonverbal expression of information. You can say "Put it here" by merely pointing, rather than by typing in a command.

Touch screens had also emerged by the time the mice appeared, providing certain attractions of their own. But fingers are larger than the small points composing a video image, and you cannot see through them. Besides, they leave greasy fingerprints. Light pens pose the same problem of obstruction, minus the fingerprints. Joysticks can be used for cursor movement, but, they don't leave the hands free to press the command and/or function keys that actually induce the computer to perform the desired tasks. Mice, it seemed, definitely deserved one's consideration.

Despite the evolutionary advance they represented, mice remained confined to the laboratories for a number of years, breeding but slowly, until Jack S. Hawley developed the first digital mouse for Xerox in 1972. The digital mouse and the modern computer are very cozy. Both speak the same binary electronic language of ones and zeros, on and off, plus and minus.

Mr. Hawley's rodent, known as the Alto Mouse, was used internally at Xerox for quite some time. It finally escaped into the world at large attached to Xerox's Star computer system. But at some $20,000 or so for the complete Star system, the electronic mouse was not about to join the biological original in most people's homes.

Meanwhile, however, Hawley opened the Mouse House, with the slogan *Purveyors of Fine Digital Mice to an Exclusive Clientele since 1975,* in Berkeley, California, and set about building a better mouse for which the world would beat a path to his door. His current mouse is called X063X. You were expecting maybe Mickey?

Manufactured under license from Xerox, the X063X uses a belly ball to sense movement and direction. Essentially, it is an upside-down trackball, similar to those used with many video arcade games. On top are three buttons that permit the user to activate various functions, such as text selection, scrolling, and graphics manipulation, all the while palming the mouse.

Other companies, such as USI International and Mouse Systems Corporation, produce optical mice, bearing names like Optomouse and M-1. These rodent renegades from some hybrid, ophthalmological world use a special grid as their turf. An optical mouse pushed back and forth across a special typewriter-paper-sized board optically senses the grid beneath its feet and translates its motion into digital impulses.

Proponents of optical mice claim that their rodents are superior to mechanical ones because they have no moving parts to break down and no ball to become gummed up. The advocates of mechanical mice, on the other hand, feel that the need for a special pad for the optical mouse to dance on limits its flexibility.

The first round in the battle of the mice has only just begun. For as the Pied Piper of personal computing plays the consumer's tune, a whole host of mice are clambering out of the circuit cellars of Silicon Valley. Neither optical nor mechanical mice may prove to be the eventual winners, though for now the leading contender for stardom is Apple's Macintosh-cum-mouse.

Almost everyone has either seen an advertisement for or otherwise heard about this personal computer. But what is working with a Macintosh really like? Every computer around these days seems to be singing the siren song "So Easy to Use." Is the Macintosh any easier and more exciting to use than the rest, as it claims to be?

For the average first-timer, hooking up the various components of a computer, sitting down at the keyboard, and actually getting the machine to do what's wanted is about as likely a series of accomplishments as building, in one's garage, a rocket capable of launching a satellite. So when a Mac, as everyone seems to refer to it, arrived for my perusal, I decided to reverse an all-American tradition. Instead of adopting the normal role of a father frustratedly trying to assemble a Christmas toy for his child by following those simple, foolproof accompanying instructions that give even graduate engineers headaches, I decided to let Tanya do the job.

A lot of computers inhabit my study, and by the time she was ten, Tanya had logged quite a number of hours testing educational software for me. But beyond turning on a computer, putting in a disk, and following the on-screen instructions, she had never had any previous experience at all with assembling the hardware.

First she pulled the computer itself out of the box on the floor. Since it weighs only seventeen pounds, this was an easy task. "Cute," she giggled, putting the rather tall but small machine on the desk.

174

A number of little white boxes with colorful, squiggly, abstract sketches on them were also pulled out of the carton. Opening one, she found a simple four-section foldout card the size of a wine menu. Commenting "This must be the instructions," she put it aside and opened the remaining boxes.

"I guess this must be the mouse . . . ," she said.

Revell, our four-year-old, piped up, "Oh, goody, maybe I can carry the mouse. It's so tiny for a boy to carry."

"I suppose I should put the keyboard in front of the computer, and there's the *boing* thing," Tanya continued, referring to the curled cable used to connect the keyboard to the computer.

With everything unpacked and the desk looking like a rummage sale at an electronics store, Tanya returned to the instructions and the larger manual enclosed with the computer, looking mostly at the pictures.

Finally the time came for action. Picking up the keyboard cable, she observed, "They don't tell you which end to plug into the computer."

That was true. After studying the cable and noting that both end connectors looked the same, she assumed it didn't make any difference which connector went where. That was also true.

In five minutes she had everything plugged together—keyboard, mouse, computer, and printer. Turning on the machine, she loaded the tutorial disk, titled A Guided Tour of Macintosh.

MacPaint and MacWrite, programs for graphics and word processing, respectively, also come with guided tours. Each of these tours combines a tutorial diskette, which puts the computer through its paces, and an instructional audio cassette to lead you through the maze. The assumption seems to be that anyone who buys a personal computer must certainly have a cassette player around. Without it, you cannot run the tutorial. That caveat aside, the hand-holding introduction provided by the guided tours should painlessly familiarize anyone with the basics of running the Macintosh in a matter of a couple of hours.

Tanya went through the first tutorial sustained by an almost uninterrupted fascination. Her initial response to the modernized Muzak in the background of the audio voiceover, "I hope this music doesn't go all the way through the tape," was replaced halfway through the MacPaint tutorial with "They should have a MacMusic program."

She was right, of course, and maybe someone will oblige. At the time of this writing, however, the software available for the Mac is fairly well limited to MacWrite, MacPaint, ThinkTank, an equation analyzer called TK! Solver, a data base manager called DB Master, and the inevitable games—Frogger, Sargon III, and so on. With its ultrahigh resolution, at least by today's personal computer standards, the Mac should make an excellent game machine. Still, the computer's display is black and white, which takes a lot away from those wedded to vivid video.

The promotional emphasis is on fun as well as ease of use, and people I've seen working with the Mac do seem to enjoy exploring its capabilities—to the point where I'm not sure whether, placed in an office setting, it would become a productive tool or a coffee break toy. When, at the mere press of a mouse ear, you can switch the words you have just written from a clean-cut Helvetica-like typeface to an ornate London or any of a number of other fonts, capturing the right look for your words can easily become as time-consuming a project, for many people, as composing the message itself. Add to this the option of inserting drawings wherever desired, and the interoffice memo may well begin to resemble a rebus.

The vying of appearance and actual content for supremacy in word processing aside, the mouse is what makes the Mac possible. The Mac mouse (why wasn't it MacMouse?) has one ear, or button, for control, a long cord to the computer for a tail, and a bellybutton ball on which the whole device slides back and forth across the desktop.

Initially, it is a bit difficult to slide the mouse around on the desk in such a fashion that the cursor arrow on the screen, whose movement the mouse controls, goes where you want it to go. Particular attention must be paid to pointing the mouse in the right direction. The "head" should always face the back of the desk. Otherwise the cursor will go off to the side when you want it to slide upwards on the screen. After half an hour of practice, however, positioning the mouse and leading it around become such second nature that the pointer seems almost an extension of one's mind.

A curious aspect of working with the electronic rodent becomes apparent when one is using the erase feature of MacPaint. The program allows a range of artistic functions for freehand drawing that encompasses a computerized spray can, a brush, a pencil, automatic shading, stippling, and other background effects. Each function is visually identified by a picture, or icon. If you want to use, say, the spray can mode, you slip the arrow cursor over the picture of the spray can and click the mouse's ear once. Then you guide the arrow to the bottom of the screen, select one of the thirty-eight different shading patterns, click again, and you are ready to spray.

If you decide you want to change some of your screen graffiti after you are done, you have only to move the cursor over the picture of an eraser, a somewhat hapless rectangular icon, to commence the deed. Watching Tanya erase a free-form picture she had drawn, however, I noticed that she pressed the mouse harder and harder on the desk as she swept the eraser across the screen. Although she was not muttering "Out, out, damned spot," it was nevertheless obvious that the kinesthesia of real-world erasing had been transferred to its video counterpart.

Erasing need not be done piecemeal. A simple double click of the mouse ear while the cursor is over the appropriate icon will clear the whole screen. Most of the Mac's applications, in fact, entail no more than a few mouse steps to carry the cursor across the screen and then a tickle of the ear or two to effect the desired results. There are times when the machine's slow reading of disks drives one up the wall, but, overall, the high-resolution Macintosh combined with the specialized mouse software represents a significant step forward in personal computer technology.

In what specific directions that step may lead us in the future is another question. After using the innovative Macintosh for a while, I can't help but wonder how much the limitations and the possibilities of personal computing, taken together, will affect the culture of our society in years to come.

For example, as MacWrite now stands, the maximum file, or document, length is about ten typed pages. That is, after you have typed in ten pages of, say, a novel, you must start a new document. It's like having to write a book none of whose chapters can be longer than ten pages. Although there are ways of getting around this limitation, they are particularly cumbersome in the case of the Mac, with its single disk drive and small memory. In actual use, MacWrite's circumscribed files pose difficulties far more trying than might at first be supposed.

Shortly after the Mac's arrival, Tanya decided to use it to compose a short story, assigned as a special school project. MacWrite features special typefaces that would allow her to design a fancy title page and cover for her "book," while MacPaint could help her in illustrating it.

The production of "Hollyhock the Cow," the story of a stray bovine in the Rocky Mountains, turned out to be both a joy and a chore. With MacPaint, Tanya drew an Elsie-like Jersey standing in a meadow of flowers. With MacWrite, she composed a twenty-page story—muttering and grumbling all the way.

The causes of her discontent were the incessant reappearance of a "Disk full" message and the concomitant need to switch disks. Every time a program disk was reinserted, the computer had to reread it. The Mac's internal memory is not large enough to store a disk's entire contents. Even though the special Mac disks provided supply a lot of data storage space, the system software and special printer software the Macintosh requires in order to run a program take up half of the available disk space, which doesn't leave that much room for the user's input. MacPaint and MacWrite together take up half of the remaining space, leaving only a quarter of the much vaunted 400K disk capacity for actual, creative use.

By two o'clock in the morning of the day the story was due, having already begged for and received an extension of her deadline, Tanya had become so frustrated over all the disk switching and all the time spent waiting for the computer to do its homework that she chucked trying to merge her picture of Elsie the cow into the text and wearily gathered up the pages of straight, albeit fancy, text to turn in later that morning. The lack of illustration knocked her grade down from an A to an A minus, and she hasn't used the Mac since.

With only 128K of RAM as its internal storage facility for programs and data to be manipulated, the original Macintosh simply is not up to the complex demands of its own unique software. The newer fat Mac, as it has been dubbed, which comes with 512K of internal memory, is the only Mac anyone should consider buying.

The Mac's single disk drive compounds the memory problem. Duplicating a disk using a single drive takes more total arm movement than picking a bushel of blueberries.

An add-on second disk drive is now available for the computer, but I question the efficacy of even this remedy. To my mind, the Mac is a machine that almost inescapably needs a hard disk in order to spare the user the frustrations of waiting. Waiting is a tedious occupation that is somehow amplified by computing. One is led to expect instantanous results from an electronic savant.

As to the much vaunted graphics capabilities of the Macintosh, yes, they really are easy to use. But most of us are not graphic artists, by any means. Thus I suspect that the majority of people looking for illustrative matter in computerland will turn, not to mouse-executed freehand drawings, but to electronic clip art of the canned, predrawn variety found in programs such as Click Art, from T/Maker, and Mac the Knife, from Miles Computing. The latest offshoot of the canned picture mania is Macinshots, from Design Loft, which allows you to select photographs digitally stored on disk of such diverse subjects as owls, Venetian gondoliers, helicopters, and President Reagan. Exactly what these will be used for leaves me guessing.

There is one place where I foresee the capabilities of the Mac, one fully equipped, that is, appearing as a godsend, and that is in the realm of schematics. A panoply of specialized Mac software devoted to true graphics applications such as engineering drawings, architectural renderings, and various similar design endeavors is being developed and should be released soon. For the rest of us, simply looking for a good word processor, spreadsheet, or data base, for instance, I don't see much need for graphics.

To me, a computer picture is neither art nor, usually, necessary for the purposes of conveying information. My negative feelings on the matter extend to all those pie charts one so frequently sees the obviously successful business executive pondering with a smile in computer advertisements. I am not at all convinced that such charts necessarily say more than a few well-chosen words could. Nevertheless, people do want pictures, or so the computer industry seems to believe, and who am I to argue with instant multimillion-dollar successes (or failures)?

Let's face it. Video games, in all their irrationality, were what first gave impetus to the personal computer. Yet the so-called graphics in such primeval arcade attractions as Pong did not merit the use of the word by even a minimalist. It's pretty hard to think of a bouncing ball and a couple of lines as much of a picture. Nevertheless, Pong was a real achievement, both technologically and, in a sense, intellectually, since it proved to be a novel way to successfully empty America's pockets of quarters.

The suspicion that graphics might actually come to dominate personal computers within this decade swept through my mind one day as I passed the game arcade in New York City's Penn Station. A herd of commuting executives had gathered around a young player whose mastery of Dragon's Lair, the first interactive video disk computer game, was obvious. The enrapturing video display had the quality of a movie cartoon, if jerkier in its sequence shifts. Visually, the difference between Pong and Dragon's Lair is the difference between playing with matchsticks at a bar and controlling the actors in a movie.

Videography on the home screen, however, has ahead of it a long and difficult passage to perfection. Not the least of the obstacles it must overcome is determining which means and methods it should use in striving toward that end. Whose graphics standards will be used? Whose disk format will be the 33-rpm record of the future, and whose the 45 and 78? So far there is no agreement on the sales and marketing approach to be taken, even in so small a thing as educating the consumer to a more graphic, and perhaps less verbal, form of expression in computing.

Mice are not the only new devices being promoted as tools appropriate to the tasks of developing on-screen graphics and manipulating data stored in a computer. Two other technologies, those of the light pen and the touch tablet, are trying to snare your processing hand as well.

The word *pen* takes on a new electronic meaning when used in conjunction with the word *light* in the anomaly *light pen*. Here is a pen that appears to be writing when, in effect, it is reading.

Even shaped like a pen, but with a small lens where the point should be, and a long umbilical cord connecting its other end to the computer, this device senses light on a video screen. It then sends signals back to the computer, which, after determining the location at which the pen is pointing on the screen, performs whatever operations the software calls for with reference to that spot.

A real honest-to-goodness regular pen can be used with almost any piece of paper. A light pen can normally be used with any video monitor, but only if the computer has light-pen-oriented software loaded. Using a light pen with ordinary software, like writing with a ballpoint on wax paper, is a useless endeavor.

Given the proper software, the modus operandi of a light pen and that of a mouse are fairly similar, although, used as a positioning device, the light pen requires a little less complex eye-hand coordination than the mouse does. When you are working with a light pen as your pointer, you are not only looking at the screen, but actually touching it with the pen. For example, you make choice number three on a menu offering six alternatives by simply pointing the pen at the number three. When you are directing the action by means of a mouse, however, your eyes are on the screen, following a cursor that moves in response to your hand, which, outside your range of vision, is sliding the mouse around on the table beside the computer.

Which of the two devices is easier to work with, the mouse or the light pen, is really a personal question, answerable only after an actual hands-on trial. Both implements are variously coordination-dependent, and which one the user finds easier to manipulate is bound to influence his or her choice, as I discovered when trying out the Edumate Light Pen, from Futurehouse.

The first step in Edumating one's computer, I learned upon unpacking the unit, is to load the software. This, according to the instructions, must be done before the light pen cord is even plugged into the designated control port of the computer.

The cord itself I found to be rather a nuisance. Hooked up to, for instance, a Commodore SX-64 portable, whose control ports are at the rear, the cord is long enough to reach the screen at the front. However, because of the tension on the cord, manipulating the light pen has all the grace of maneuvering a ballpoint with a five-pound weight on its nonwriting end. Still, I was pleased to note that the light pen does function on the diminutive five-inch screen of the portable. One of the problems with these devices is their insensitivity to fine resolution, and I had been a bit dubious about its ability to function on such a small screen.

Using a full-sized monitor placed next to the computer instead of its own built-in little one relieved some of the tension on the cord. But I still found myself holding the light pen as if it were a wand, to compensate for the weight of the cord.

Even more annoying was the fact that, in order to activate the pen, one must hold down either the F7 function key or the left-hand shift key. This means that both hands are occupied in managing the device, one on the pen, the other on the keyboard. Try doing it if you're a lefty. A switch mounted on the pen itself, in the manner of the ears on the electronic mouse, would have been far more convenient.

The starter software included in the Edumate package has four parts. These are of variable interest to the light-penmanship practitioner.

182

The first program, a drawing routine for freehand sketching, takes full advantage of the Commodore's designated color keys. For example, pressing the key for the number one allows you to draw in black or orange, number two in white or brown, and so on. But where the light pen offers the advantage of color and economy, the Mac mouse used in conjunction with MacPaint offers far more detail and flexibility, albeit in black and white. Though not directly comparable, these differences are important in making a choice between the two implements.

Pen Music, a second Edumate program, is for composing. Touch the dot next to the D-sharp on the screen, and that will be the note produced by the machine. Even with eight octaves and three waveforms, however, the program is very limited. It is more a demonstration of possibilities than a full-scale composition program. Equally circumscribed is the three-dimensional tick-tack-toe thrown into the package, which is no more and no less than the simple game designated by the name. The last program in the series is a handful of utilities allowing you to format a disk automatically, run a program, and activate other options, using the light pen rather than the keyboard.

A more advanced program called Peripheral Vision, from the same company, allows one not only to draw freehand, but to select from among various computer-drawn shapes as well. Again, for drawing, I found using the pen to be a more clumsy undertaking than I had expected. Because of the angle and distance of the penpoint from the image behind the thick glass screen, I often ended up putting a line in the wrong place.

As in the acquisition of any motor skill, my efforts would improve with time, I assume. Certainly the pen itself is a clever and inexpensive enough device. Even so, I can't help but wonder, first of all, whether sufficient usable software will be produced to take advantage of this type of peripheral and, second, whether such a pen is really needed and convenient or whether it is merely another clever solution in search of a problem.

Clever solutions that never seem to find a substantial problem to solve are plentiful in the world of personal computing. I particularly remember an early one called digital foam. Developed by a backyard inventor whose name I fear I have forgotten, digital foam was the subject of the lead article in *ROM* magazine's first issue. Resembling pieces of a used inner tube from a DC-3, this foam had the remarkable property of being able to convert real-world information directly into the binary data used by modern computers.

In theory, then, a pad made of this material would enable one to sign one's name on it, say, and have the computer recognize the signature instantly, as well as display it on screen. The foam could also be used as a weight sensor for a scale or a nonmechanical touch-sensitive switch. The potential uses of the material seemed myriad. Yet when *ROM* ran a contest to unearth the best application for this curious material, we had numerous requests for samples, followed by numerous letters saying how great the stuff was, but no one propounded a single practical application for it. No products embodying digital foam appear to have made their way to market since.

The memory of digital foam, however, bounced immediately to the forefront of my consciousness on first seeing touch tablets. Koala Technologies' KoalaPad and Chalk Board's Power Pad use a touch-sensitive membrane, a sandwich of firm plastic material in which are embedded switches that become activated when pressure is applied to the membrane, either with a stylus, or inkless pen, or with one's finger. On the KoalaPad, the sensitive surface is four-and-a-quarter inches square. On the much larger Power Pad, it measures twelve square inches. Neither surface is as sensitive as the original digital foam was, however, and neither surface is capable of its gradated sensing. Still, both permit reasonably smooth lines to be drawn.

The bigger pad is easier to work on and offers better resolution, facilitating more detailed drawings. On the other hand, some users prefer the smaller unit because it occupies less desk space in an environment already crowded with peripherals and cables.

Besides being so dissimilar in size, the KoalaPad and the

Power Pad differ functionally in that the Power Pad uses digital circuitry rather than the analog technology employed by the KoalaPad and most other devices of this kind. In the case of an analog-based tablet, if you touch the pad at two points simultaneously, the computer will choose one of the two, more or less at will, as its input. It can accept no more than a single signal at a time. By contrast, digital switches, of which the Power Pad has 14,400 buried in its membrane, are discrete. Each point on a digital pad can be individually discerned by the computer.

To illustrate, if you put a music keyboard overlay on a digital tablet, you can play several notes at once, a complete chord, for example. An analog equivalent of the pad would allow you to play only one note at a time, as in practicing scales.

A more homely illustration of the difference between the two tablets can be achieved by simply pressing your hand against them. The image appearing on the screen in response to the pressure on the digital pad will be that of your whole hand, whereas the analog switches will give you an impression of only a few scattered dots or stray lines.

Should your hand wander off the drawing surface of the KoalaPad, it will discover two buttons, similar to those found on the electronic mouse. These buttons are employed with the drawing programs to perform such functions as switching from a sketch you are working on to a menu. Click once and the menu appears. Select, say, a color, press the button again, and you are returned to the drawing mode so that you can shade in the color chosen.

Unlike the KoalaPad, the Power Pad has no need of buttons. By virtue of its digital nature and larger size, parts of its drawing surface are simply designated as soft keys, or specific areas of the pad assigned the various tasks necessary to operate a program. For example, the upper right-hand corner of the tablet might be marked Menu on a particular overlay, the plastic sheet with imprinted commands that accompanies a touch tablet software selection and is laid on top of the pad while you are actually running the program. Touch this spot and the menu would automatically be called up on screen.

Drawing programs represent the primary initial thrust of the software available for both the Power Pad and the Koala-Pad, although the manufacturer of the latter is now marketing a sedate, gray version of the tablet called KT2010 for the sedate, gray executive office. Sold along with Speed Key software and overlays for such programs as Lotus 1-2-3, Super-Calc, MultiPlan, and WordStar, this executive pad and software allow one to enter complex commands condensing as many as eighty keystrokes to a single stab of the pen at a designated spot on its surface.

More typical of the pad software available is Island Software's MicroIllustrator, whose program was written by Steve Dompier, that selfsame software designer who made the original Altair play "Daisy"—old programmmers never die, they just keep writing more code.

MicroIllustrator offers capabilities not found in traditional pen-and-paper graphics media. For instance, you can draw a design on your pad using a stylus, which is essentially simply a pointed stick, but one that enables you to execute a more detailed picture than you would be able to achieve with your fingers, although they are equally usable for the job. Then, using the FILL command, you can have the computer shade in designated areas for you, painting the sky blue or a tree green. The command CIRCLE will induce the computer to draw this shape automatically in any size you specify. DISC will execute the same maneuver, but here the circle will fill itself in with any color you choose. FRAME will make squares and rectangles for you. ERASE will do just that as you rub the stylus across the pad as if it were an eraser.

The most intriguing command in the repertoire of Micro-Illustrator, however, is probably MAGNIFY. This directive enlarges the screen image on which you are working seven times, making it possible for you to zoom in on a portion of a drawing and redo it, if you so desire, dot by dot. The magnifying function, similar to that found in the graphics editors of some type-design software, is particularly useful in blending shades of colors and softening the outlines of objects.

Even with all the aids supplied by such relatively advanced graphics software, however, pictures produced by computer

186

are still far less elegant than those drawn freehand with pencil and paper. Nor can the current crop of personal computers offer television-quality, much less true photographic quality, images.

The resolution presently available not only fails to do justice to the artistic muse, but sometimes makes a muddle of the touch-screen approach to communicating with the computer as well. Screen resolution is bound to be the next area of improvement in the resources of personal computing. However, its refinement will probably hinder, rather than help, the efficacy of touch screens.

At first glance, the touch screen, which is actually activated not by touch, but by your finger breaking small light beams like those of the old electric-eye-operated doors, might seem the ultimate alternative to the keyboard. So it must have seemed to the people at Hewlett-Packard when they designed the HP-150, which tries to incorporate the keyboard functions, at least in part, into the computer's special touch screen.

At nine inches diagonally, however, the screen is not adequate to the tasks assigned it, even when the characters are as clear and crisp as they are on its green phosphorus screen. When one is running a program like VisiCalc using the touch screen, poking at the desired number to get the cursor on top of it often results in positioning the cursor to one side of or below the number instead. One becomes pretty adept at fine-tuning one's fingers after a while. All the same, I found the performance of the touch screen, at least with the VisiCalc software, less than satisfactory. And I do not have fat fingers.

The so-called soft keys do not similarly fall short of providing the right touch. I am not sure why they are called soft keys in this instance, since here they are small rectangular boxes of light appearing at the bottom of the screen, and thus are as hard as the screen itself. In any case, there are eight of them, and their functions are continually changing. When you first power up the computer, two are blank and the other six are variously labeled *Start Applic, Set Date and Time, Reread Discs, HELP,* and so on. They are all fairly self-explanatory and easy to use. Touch *Set Date and Time,* for example,

187

and you are greeted with a request to type in those particulars, after which you are returned to the first screen. Few things could be simpler.

To load the software, let's say the word processing program WordStar, you merely slip the disk into the drive, touch *Start Applic*, wait a few seconds for the name WordStar to appear, touch *Start Applic* again, and WordStar is ready to run. You will find that the eight soft keys have now been relabeled with such WordStar functions as *Open Document, Print Options,* and so on. The keys will be relabeled again and again as needed during the running of the program.

WordStar, frankly, is far from being my favorite word processing program. But WordStar is what came with the HP-150 I received, so, to put the computer touch screen to the test of actual use, I opened a file and proceeded to peck away, typing my random thoughts: "This is a real pain in many ways. Why? It looks so good in theory. . . . For one thing, the manual is really poor. It's almost a crime to send it out with what appears to be such a fine piece of technology. The instructions might read as a technologist's delight, but for the nontechnical consumer they are a discouraging turnoff."

The touch-screen system itself is simple to master. Any complicated control codes can be replaced at a mere touch of the soft keys. But, when all is said and done, the touch screen simply is not as effective as it might be because the resolution is accurate to only a two-character width. A larger screen with larger type could have refined it to a more useful one-character resolution. Regretfully I put the disks away. In the end, the HP-150 had proved to be the computer I wanted to fall in love with at first touch, but didn't.

After using an innovative and imaginative computer product or peripheral for a while, the novelty of it wears off. That's when its shining benefits may begin to seem a little tarnished with reality. Perhaps, after all, they were never as great as they were claimed to be.

So the sparkle of the light pen may dim, the touch tablet and the touch screen alike join digital foam in oblivion, the mouse share the fate of the mammoth. Who knows? Maybe function and cursor keys and the mundane keyboard will continue to reign supreme. Certainly Apple's decision not to put any cursor keys at all on the Macintosh seems a mistake. Mouse or no mouse, sometimes, and for some things, it's just plain easier to use the cursor keys.

Then again, maybe the battle for the hearts of personal computer customers will switch fronts, from hands to feet. Why shouldn't a foot-operated control switch, similar to that of a sewing machine treadle, be used to operate the movement of the cursor on the screen? It would make a lot of sense to use both hands and feet when computing, as when driving a car. Come to think of it, I wonder if maybe that's what Apple is hinting at in suggesting that you "Take a Macintosh out for a test drive."

Again, the best approach of all might be just to tell your computer what to do and have it instantly obey. Wouldn't it be nice to turn on the computer and be greeted by, instead of the infernal A>, a pleasant voice saying, "I'm ready. What is your desire?"

11: Never Say "Forget It"

In pondering what changes computers will engender in the manners and mores of our culture, nowhere do I find them more imponderable, perhaps, than as they affect our auditory lives. More than once, upon being greeted by the chirps of the now pervasive audio chip, have I sibilantly hissed, "Shut up." Not normally prone to use the phrase in conversing with people, I find it increasingly expressive of my sentiments when confronted with soniferous machines.

The once obedient but mute tools of man are becoming more and more vocal, to hardly anyone's real benefit that I can see. Do we need a talking dashboard to remind us to buckle our seat belts or to tell us that our car is low on oil? If Detroit wishes to improve the dashboard, why does it not simply replace the red idiot warning lights currently dotting the panel with the real gauges formerly found there, so that one will be able once more to monitor the engine's performance *before* something goes wrong?

My auditive ire was recently roused to new heights by a lately released talking alarm clock. The device can be set, according to its proud purveyors, to announce the time verbally every minute. The ad they devised for it does not suggest purchasing it for someone sight-impaired, to whom it could obviously be of use, but rather as an all-around handy household appliance no bedroom should be without. Surely such a contrivance punctuating our day-to-day lives would be nothing short of an electronic version of the old Chinese water torture. As far as I'm concerned, its perpetrator should be chained for eternity to a bed in a room full of such clocks, each one set to announce at every moment a different time.

Pandora's box of electronic gadgetry, once opened, is exceedingly hard to close. Just try, nowadays, to buy a decent wind-up alarm clock with a suitably slow, relaxing ticktock and a functional, but at least moderately mellifluous, alarm.

Revenge is probably less than a decade away, however. Sometime within the next ten years, when you tell your personal computer to be quiet, *it* will have to listen—and respond, probably by going into a silent electronic sulk.

Computerized speech recognition is a much-ballyhooed technology slowly emerging from the dimly lit corners of the electronics industry's laboratories. Whether it will ever reach the stage of perfection envisioned by its proponents is another matter. Creating an audio chip, one capable of producing various sounds, including, with proper programming, those of the human voice, is a considerable technical achievement. Yet it pales beside the task of developing speech recognition in computers, at least on a level where the machines will be capable of distinguishing the vernacular word voiced by any given individual from the myriad of other words the sounds might propose if taken out of the context in which used, or if spoken by someone else.

Voice generation, for all the technical triumphs the chip that crowned its hardware evolution represented, is today not much more than canned sound. A supersophisticated version of the now commonplace cassette or stereo recording, it is circumscribed by the limitations of its software to somewhat mundane uses. This is not to say that it will never do more, but merely to point out that the basic technical deed is done.

191

Voice transmission, as over a telephone, and even compression, which allows more words to be sent in a given time span, are equally narrowly defined areas of technological endeavor, serving more or less as interpreters, translating sound into digital impulses and converting them back again.

Speech recognition, on the other hand, entails a broad mélange of arts and sciences. Not only chip design, acoustic theory, and signal processing, but linguistics and probability theory as well, are involved. It is, in truth, the most difficult aspect of voice processing, for it probably requires the completion of that seemingly hopeless task, the development of artificial intelligence. Only then could it reach the universal state where anyone at all giving a machine a verbal command could have it understood, no matter what the syntax or the accent—and regardless of a stuffy nose, a state rendering the current generation of crude voice recognition systems deaf.

The understanding of speech does indeed require intelligence. Not only are the meanings and the order of the words used significant, but interpretive decisions may be required for their comprehension as well. Many words are acoustically ambiguous, and can be grasped correctly only within their context. That is a central problem not easily circumvented in the designing of voice-activated machinery.

Interestingly enough, even humans understand less of what is spoken than one might think. According to a study by I. Pollack and J. M. Pickett, *The Intelligibility of Excerpts from Conventional Speech*, 20 to 30 percent of the words in a recorded conversation cannot be understood by an individual when played back as single words, even when that same individual understood each and every word of the conversation as a whole. The information needed to interpret a word is often found, not solely in the term itself, but rather distributed in part among adjoining words. *Apple* has a meaning quite different from that of the word as heard in the phrase *rotten apple*, and maybe quite different from that which it had only a decade ago.

Inducing speech recognition in a machine, then, is not akin to teaching a child a language. It is a matter of first building a "child" capable of all the auditory finesse and linguistic analysis entailed in listening, and only then teaching it a language. The immensity, if not audacity, of the task is enough to make a mere mortal shrug his shoulders and seek out his trustiest fishing rod. But the computer industry remains serenely undaunted.

At least a dozen new companies dedicated to the marketing of speech recognition systems have sprung up over recent years. As many have already been relegated to that great toxic scrap heap in the silicon sky. Even so, voice recognition products capable of responding to isolated utterances, that is, to single words or short phrases carefully enunciated and scrupulously separated by well-defined pauses, have come on the market. More advanced modules capable of recognizing words, however differently they are voiced, and interpreting their semantic meaning in the context of normal, diaphonic conversation will not, in my opinion, be available until well into the year 2000—if ever.

Whatever degree of relative sophistication a present-day speech recognition system has, its structure is basically the same as that of any of its contemporaries. It must have a hearing aid, first of all, and then it must be able to sort incoming sounds into patterns recognizable by its electronic "intellect."

A microphone picks up the sounds, a device called a band-pass filter is used to allow certain sounds to enter while excluding others, letting the relevant ones pass through to the computer unattenuated, and an analog-to-digital converter takes the analog sound waves of our speech and converts them into digital signals the computer can process. These are the constituents of the sound analyzer portion of a recognition system, and they are the easy parts to devise.

The other element of the system is the classifier, which does exactly what its name implies. Breaking the sounds as they are received down into manipulable components, proceeding at a constant rate of, say, 100 segments per second, it then classifies them. The processes involved are really too complex for anyone not making a career of voice recognition research to strive to understand. But by way of background, there are two predominant methods of achieving the desired results.

One form of classification employs a matrix, with elapsed

time along one axis and sound frequency along the other. Comparisons are made between series of known sounds similarly broken down. For example, your voiced word "help" spoken into the microphone would be compared with your previous input of the same word.

A more complicated method of analysis is referred to as dynamic programming. Structured so that it recognizes the same sound even when that sound is of a different duration and uttered under different circumstances, it permits matching a slow, jocular "Hel-l-l-p-p-p" with the sharp "Help!" of fear. As you might suspect, the technology involved is much more intricate than that of the first method. For our purposes, suffice it to say that teaching a computer to recognize Beethoven's Fifth, with its regularity of sonic patterns, from two different recordings is a lot easier than teaching it to understand two different children asking if they can go out and play.

But if some of the obstacles facing computerized voice recognition seem almost insurmountable, they have in no way deterred researchers and would-be manufacturers from their assault on this Gordian knot. Texas Instruments, probably the current leader in the arcane field of electronic speech, has even brought voice recognition to the world of personal computing.

The Texas Instruments Speech Command System, SCS for short, greets the observer with a rather intimidating price tag. One's first reaction is apt to be, "I could buy another whole computer for that!"

Well, another whole computer is what the Speech Command System amounts to, in fact. The computing power and sophistication required are such that a full-sized piggyback board—two boards sandwiched together in order to use but one slot in the computer's expansion chassis—is part and parcel of the system.

Despite its somewhat imposing and complicated mien, the Speech Command System is surprisingly simple to install and run. To make your machine truly conversant, however, will take considerable time.

The first thing I discovered upon removing the cover of a

194

Texas Instruments Professional Computer, that company's version of the IBM PC, to install the SCS hardware, was that, with its excess avoirdupois, this fat board would not fit into either of the outside slots. Also, since the computer already had a communications board, I had to throw the old one out, figuratively speaking. The SCS system includes every conceivable communications task, from voice recognition to dictation recording and smart phone features.

With the new board in place, I proceeded to the conversational gadgetry, attaching the speaker cables—so I could listen—and plugging in the lightweight microphone headset—so the machine could listen. Then I slipped the diagnostic disk into drive A, fervently hoping it would verify that everything was functioning properly.

The diagnostic disk in this particular case contains programs that permit the computer not only to check out the keyboard, video display, memory, and other basics, but also to test its master's voice quality. I must say it was a bit disconcerting to hear the computer discoursing with me in the resonant tones of a cigarette commercial voice-over.

Actually, of course, it wasn't discoursing at all. One should probably restrain oneself from the anthropomorphizing that tends to occur under such semiextraordinary circumstances. What it was doing was playing back a prerecorded voice stored on the floppy disk.

Most people, myself included, tend to think of disks as mute storehouses of those mysterious command sequences that compose the software we use when running the computer. We do not associate floppies with voices or other sounds. Yet, given the right hardware, floppy disks are quite capable of tonal recording, resembling in that instance those digital stereo records now making their way to the consumer market.

Once all the installed hardware had been approved by the diagnostic disk and the computer had cleared its prerecorded throat, the machine and I proceeded to the speech recognition software itself. This consists of yet two more floppy disks, one to direct the machinery, one to direct the conversation.

The first disk, the Speech Command System Software, is to

the newly installed circuit board what the operating system software, or DOS, is to the computer itself, namely, that which transforms it from an expensive paperweight into a machine capable of performing the desired applications. The Speech Command System Software specifically provides for voice recognition, voice storage, and voice playback as well as various integrated telephone functions like automatic dialing. It also turns your computer into a programmable telephone answering machine, a dictation machine, or, for that matter, a digital hi-fi, though I don't foresee the imminent release of either Jackson or Janáček on five-and-a-quarter-inch disk.

The other disk in the Speech Command System package carries the mysterious-sounding designation Transparent Keyboard. Being a floppy, it is obviously neither a keyboard nor, in the ordinary sense of the word, transparent. Names aside, however, this is the software that translates your voice into digital signals for the computer. It does this by making an individual voiceprint for each word you plan to use in a given application. These voiceprints are the sonic equivalent of fingerprints—and just as unique to an individual.

The Transparent Keyboard comes with built-in vocabularies for seven popular applications programs: EasyWriter II, EasySpeller II, PFS:Report, PFS:File, Lotus 1-2-3, Multiplan, and NLX Dow Jones. It also includes the verbal cues needed to operate MS-DOS and MS BASIC orally. In addition, it allows you to enter any vocabulary words of your own choosing into the computer's mind.

I chose EasyWriter II as my pilot program. While it is not among my favorite word processing packages, I was anxious to start bossing my computer around, and a word processor seemed the logical choice for one who deals more in words than in numbers or other structural building-blocks. Easy-Writer II happens to be the word processor for which the Speech Command System provides a predefined vocabulary.

Using any of the SCS-allied programs with the Texas Instruments voice recognition system entails first duplicating the applications disk you want to use and then adding to it the voiceprint software from the Texas Instruments diskette.

196

But the interlacing procedure is simple enough so that one need merely follow the tutorial and on-screen instructions in order to effect it.

Having a hard disk available, at this point I transferred everything onto it, since stowing all the working pieces you need together on hard disk considerably expedites the running of a program. Now I was ready to begin training the computer to my voice.

The first step in the phonological education of the computer is achieved with the aid of a calibration program. This adjusts the gain, or relative strength, of your voice as received by the microphone. Mindful of certain well-publicized bloopers made by persons testing microphones, I simply said "Hello" half a dozen times and typed in, as requested, the number 13, representing the gain registered by the computer. Once set, the gain need not be recalibrated unless you move your computer or suddenly surround your desk with, let's say, lush plants, changing the acoustic environment.

The next step in the speech recognition exercise is to "enroll" your voice, one specific word at a time. Up to fifty words may be used in any one vocabulary. If that quantity is not enough for your purposes, additional vocabularies can be added, but they cannot be linked. It's like having fifty lines on a page. If you need more, you can always go on to another page, though you can't continue your conversation from one page to the next.

Since my chosen test program, EasyWriter II, required only twenty-seven words, and those were already provided for me, I simply began reading them off the screen and into the headset microphone. "Acknowledge . . . ruler . . . help" (that last one my own favorite), and so on.

I was almost finished when Genevieve walked in with the startled question, "Dad, why are you talking to that computer?"

Spurred to a quick-witted defense of my sanity, I sat her down and entered her voiceprints for the same vocabulary. Interestingly enough, the computer responded better to her voice than to mine. After entering the vocabulary, one is to run a closeness of fit test, which consists of reiterating the vocabulary. This time the computer matches the spoken words against the previously recorded voiceprints. Rated on a scale of one to ten, most of my matches were in the barely acceptable two to four range. Genevieve's averaged eight.

The reason for this auditory discrepancy has, I think, a lot to do with psychology. One of the more difficult tasks to be found in the contemporary world is discoursing naturally with a computer. Adults tend to speak to the machine as if to a child in need of explanation or a foreigner in search of directions. Youngsters, on the other hand, tend to jabber on as usual.

Colds also produce their share of sonic havoc. Having carefully tutored the computer in its requisite EasyWriter vocabulary, I one day found the machine barely more responsive to me than to a mute. The traditional fall cold, considerately brought home from school by the girls, had rendered my voice perhaps half an octave lower and somewhat more fluid in its enunciation.

The machine would accept some of my comments and not others. Then, inexplicably, it would listen to a word that had previously fallen on deaf electronic ears.

When it comes to idiosyncrasies unexplainable to the layman, those of a computerized speech recognition system are hard to beat. Among other things, you are never quite certain what command you are giving the computer. Saying "one" or "print" does not necessarily mean that the computer hears the word as "one" or "print." Also the fine-tuning of electronic phonetics simply has not reached the point where, for example, "three" and "tee" are totally and infallibly separate at all times to a micro's hearing aid.

Quite apart from such whimsicalities, I'm not sure that, say, verbally instructing a computer to delete a block of text is really any faster or more convenient than pressing a couple of keys to elicit the same response. Where an oral system of command does save time is in the employment of a single spoken phrase, such as "Call Fred," to activate a macro, a miniprogram containing a whole string of commands.

The construction of macros is something the Texas Instruments Speech Command System Software specifically provides for, allowing you to define your own words and phrases using special commands listed in the manual. Unless you have worked with computers for some time and have designed macros before, you are likely to find the business of stringing commands together a bit complex. However, a day's struggle with the appendices in the SCS manual should start you on your way.

Having macros on hand simplifies the putting together of proposals, statements, accounts, and other documents calling for material to be filled in. Halfway through the drafting of an inventory report, for example, you can instruct your computer to call Fred, or whomever you have specified in your macro, for the latest figures needed to complete the presentation. The computer will start dialing while you keep working on the spreadsheet, which remains up on screen. Once a connection has been made, you can ask Fred for the requisite data and enter it as he gives it to you, all without interruption.

As things now stand, even though the Speech Command System enables you to request your computer verbally to make a call for you, you do have to press a key to hang up. But this step could be modified. Since the hardware for the system has a built-in clock, the software could be customized to break a connection after thirty seconds of silence or so. Then again, if you spend a lot of time chatting with your computer, it might think you're still talking to Fred.

A significant distinction should be made between using a speech recognition system for word processing and using it for number processing, I decided, after training the Speech Command System to identify my spoken commands for Lotus 1-2-3 functions as well as for EasyWriter. Working verbally with spreadsheet software was quite different from talking to a word processor. Of the two, the spreadsheet offered much more opportunity for verbal input. While the SCS system can be used as a dictating machine, and while it can send prerecorded messages from Big Brother to all his subordinates via telephone at any preset time—indeed, the computer will keep dialing the assigned number until it gets through, no matter what—you cannot dictate a letter and have the computer convert it directly into print. Verbal communication in

199

word processing is limited to such matters as setting headers and inserting paragraph breaks—in other words, to the twenty-seven basic control commands by which you run the program.

In the case of a spreadsheet, on the other hand, the data most often entered consists of the numbers zero through nine. If a computer can be made to recognize those ten words, a great deal of actual data can be entered verbally.

Then too, frequently used categories, such as a tax rate, can be defined as part of the SCS vocabulary. For example, using Lotus 1-2-3, I defined cell A14, that is, the intersection of row A and column 14, as the place on my spreadsheet where the tax rate figure belonged. After that, no matter where on the spreadsheet I was working, whenever I wanted to enter a new tax rate figure, I simply said "tax rate," and the computer obligingly moved the cursor to A14.

With the cursor automatically on the spot, I then told the computer the new rate to be entered, verbalizing each number as a discrete entity. One must say "Five, two," for instance, not "Fifty-two." In went the information.

A mouse-type pointing device to use in conjunction with the dictated numbers would be convenient, I think. Ferreting out the desired cell by means of the roving rodent and then telling the computer verbally what to put there might appreciably increase the speed with which numeric data could be entered. It would also solve that age-old, fidgety problem of what to do with one's hands while one's mouth is running.

The limitations and drawbacks of current speech recognition systems notwithstanding, the technology forges ahead. International Research Development, a market research firm in Connecticut, estimates that speech recognition system sales as a whole will have increased from $25 million in 1984 to $270 million by the end of 1987. Given the propensity of electronics hardware to drop in price, this appraisal suggests a staggering growth of such systems. And you thought the office was noisy now?

At the personal computer level, speech recognition remains for the most part a novelty, the one notable exception being as an aid to the handicapped, for many of whom it can spell

the difference between isolation and computer-assisted interaction. Who is to say, however, what the merging of voice and
data will bring to fruition within the next few years? It may
well be that someday in the not too distant future you will
find yourself sitting at your computer exclaiming in frustration, "Oh, forget it!"—and the machine, taking your words
quite literally, will obediently return its memory to the pristine state in which it was when purchased.

12: Reach Out and Touch Someone— Anyone at All

In the early history of personal computing, when having a machine meant begging, borrowing, or stealing time on a huge multimillion-dollar mainframe, the pursuit became inexorably entwined with telephone communications. Software hackers at MIT and other universities were busy tapping into the telephone company's long lines, exploring the programs behind the switching systems and routing patterns of what was then Ma Bell. Hardware hackers like Steve Wozniak, later to cofound Apple Computer, were busy supplementing their income by building and selling blue boxes, digital devices that could be used to make unlimited "free" telephone calls. One of the august accomplishments of the period consisted of directing a telephone call around the world to ring the instrument in the room next door.

The link between computers and telecommunications is not surprising. Their common domain is information, after all.

Considering that the one, the computer, processes it and the other, the telephone, transmits it, their technological interconnection seems almost inevitable, the more so since telephony began switching over in the seventies from the analog transmission characterizing its origins to the digital technology underlying today's computers.

Even now, however, despite the almost lock-step growth of the two industries, telecommunications remains arcane. In some ways, its operating procedures are more standardized than those governing, say, software routines. Yet, for someone uninitiated in its rites, inducing a computer to deal by telephone with another computer can be a crowning achievement in frustration.

First of all, there is the matter of selecting a modem, the device that allows the computer to communicate with its distant cohorts. The modem must be compatible with the computer itself, naturally. But what other attributes need it have?

By the time you have reached the stage in computing where you are considering buying a modem, you are well aware of the fact that the acquisition of software follows unrelentingly the acquisition of hardware. Your modem will need the appropriate software.

You are also conversant with cables. You will probably need two of these, one to connect the modem to the computer, the other to connect it to the telephone line.

Invariably, one of the components or connectors you purchase will not work with or fit the others. Why, I had often asked myself over the years of looking at modems, can't someone bring out a complete communications package, all in one box, simple enough for a child to hook up and run? That way, there might be a slim chance of my getting it all put together right the first time around. Ever since building the Sol, I had felt an ambivalence to electronic things that came in bits and pieces, even the bigger bits and pieces of the newer computer components.

So when I saw an ad for Novation's Access 1-2-3, from Novation, Inc., that claimed the package included everything required to enable an IBM PC to start running up the telephone bills, I was cautiously intrigued. I ordered one. On its arrival, I gave Tanya the box, drafting her for the installation project.

By now, ten-year-old Tanya had not only played a lot of computer games and run a fair amount of educational software, but assembled computer systems by connecting the components as well. However, she had never before tackled the actual computer itself as an electronic entity, from the inside out.

The first thing she discovered was that the PC1200B modem that came with the package was an internal model, one of those intimidating green circuit boards replete with chips, colorful resistors, and all the other gut paraphernalia of modern electronic circuitry. The advantage of an internal modem is that it reduces clutter and cable spaghetti on the desk. The disadvantage is that if you ever buy a different computer, you may have to buy a new modem as well.

The tradeoff, in my opinion, is weighted on the side of the internal device. One doesn't purchase a new computer every six months, after all. Besides, were the old one to be sold, the inclusion of a modem would be more apt than not to invite a higher price.

Tanya, however, was not so sure about this reasoning. Her awed reaction to the internal modem was, "You mean I have to take the computer apart?"

"Read the instructions," I replied.

She did, at least enough of them to make a beginning. Then off she set toward her room in search of screwdrivers. (When in doubt, check under the bed. Almost anything can be found there.) Next, to make doubly certain before she started that nothing was left connected, Tanya proceeded to unplug everything, including the monitor and the printer, from both the wall outlets and the back of the computer.

The screws at the rear of the IBM PC/XT presented no problem for her. The bulky case, however, slides off with a little less than grace, particularly if your hands are small. I pitched in.

Suddenly, with the chassis unsheathed, Tanya was at the heart of the computing world. Expansion slots, transformers, mother boards, daughter boards, and all the other innards of the electronic brain were exposed.

The installation manual inquired whether the computer had a serial card. Tanya, in turn, asked me, which was reasonable enough, since it was my computer.

The answer being yes, the manual informed her that she would have to make a hardware adjustment to the modem. Besides inserting the awesome board correctly into the computer console, she would have to change some connections.

That was no big deal, but if you've never handled electronic components before. . . . To make sure she wasn't full of static electricity, Tanya touched the radiator—three times. She is as nervous about electricity as I am. Then, following the instructions, she removed a small, red plastic cap covering a pair of pins labeled (fortunately clearly) J6 on the board, and placed it on two pins labeled J7. Next, the jumper on E4 went to W4.

"That's all?" she remarked when she was finished. She seemed disappointed that she would not have the opportunity to tinker with any of the other tiny parts of the modem.

After removing the appropriate slot cover from the back of the computer, Tanya connected black, green, and white wires from the Novation board to matching ones on the computer's speaker. Permitting auditory monitoring of the computer's calls as they are being placed, amplifying the dial tones, dialing, and busy signals, the speaker connection is a handy feature.

Finally, the modem board itself, complete with its umbilical cords, was put into the slot nearest the speaker, pushed down firmly, and screwed into place. The XT's cover was replaced, and the cables from the telephone wall outlet and the telephone were both plugged in. The two-cable phone connection is another convenient feature of the Novation package. It allows you to leave the telephone plugged in to the computer, ready to be used even when the machine is turned off, rather than disconnecting the modem and reconnecting the telephone whenever it is needed by humans.

The installation had gone smoothly and according to the illustrations in the manual. Apparently the instructions really

205

were clear enough for a child to follow. Reconnecting all the peripherals she had detached in her concern for her safety and plugging in the computer's power cord, Tanya took a deep breath and turned on the computer. Had she killed it?

The familiar memory check came on screen. Everything was fine.

Slipping in the Crosstalk XVI disk, the communications software included in the Novation package, Tanya entered XTALK, as directed by the start-up instructions, and was met by a status display encompassing a bewildering array of options having to do with communications parameters, filter settings, key settings, and so on. They covered most of the screen.

At the bottom, room had been left for a commmand line. There Tanya entered PO2, for input/output port number 2, matching the software's configuration to the hardware change she had made as directed by the manual, before I even had a chance to say anything. Then, after a cursory examination of the Crosstalk section on running the program for the first time, which, incidentally, is the only portion of the instruction manual (as opposed to the installation manual) that is clear sailing for the beginner, Tanya entered the command NU, for new-user information.

"Enter new phone number," she was told.

"Hey, that's supposed to be 'Enter number to dial' " was her immediate response.

That was indeed the way the manual had stated the command. Mumbling about the lack of precision in the world of computers, she entered the telephone number given as an example. The computer dialed away. It failed, however, to induce the telephone at the other end to ring. And failed. And failed.

Here was a classic instance of the traditional computer bind wherein you get something running but it doesn't work, usually because the operating instructions were not clear. After some time, Tanya discovered, well hidden in the manual, a reference to the fact that if you are situated in a remote area, such as ours, that still uses a rotary telephone system, an *I* must precede a number.

Entering the *I* still didn't get her a connection.

206

This time she dialed Novation's help line—manually. One of the technicians, Eddy Turnier, explained that because we had a rotary, or pulse, telephone, the computer needed a longer interval in which to make a connection. He told her how to increase the allotted time for dialing.

Tanya changed the appropriate parameter, tried again, and jumped for joy when the computer got through. She spent the rest of the evening inducing her new electronic tool to call up, variously, The Source, a NASA information service, and other computers throughout the land.

NASA, we discovered, had not even known about the computerized service listing its activities until I happened to mention it in an article. They telephoned Tanya to get the number. In case you are curious too, it's (301) 344-9156, and the reason NASA had not been aware of its existence was that the service in question is not an official government agency, but rather one of a myriad of private computerized bulletin boards.

Operated by what is referred to as a SYSOP, or system operator, a public access bulletin board is simply a telecommunications version of the old supermarket bulletin board. Anyone with a personal computer and a telephone line can start one.

There are hundreds, probably even thousands, of these privately operated systems in current operation, forming a great computer underground. From the Avionics Interest Group to the Pacific Medical Bulletin Board, there are electronic news-and-notes exchanges to serve specialty interests of almost every description. There are IBM-, Apple-, and Commodore-oriented ones. There are game boards, particularly popular, like the one for Space Diplomacy in New York. There are plain and simple freewheeling boards, electronic gathering places for disembodied minds, where anyone can leave a message and see who answers it.

All these public access exchanges have led up to a very interesting law case, one which may well make its way, in the old-fashioned written manner of case law, to the Supreme Court. The question at issue is who becomes responsible for what appears on a bulletin board.

The well-publicized case at issue is that of a Los Angeles

Computerized Bulletin Board, or CBB, operator by the name of Thomas G. Tcimpidis, who had his equipment seized by the police and now faces criminal charges for "knowingly and willfully publishing" telephone credit card numbers on his bulletin board. Tcimpidis claims that he did not publish the numbers, that someone else called his bulletin board and entered the information into the computer.

The issue is of no minor importance. Large corporations sponsoring electronic information retrieval utilities, such as CompuServe, The Source, and the Times Mirror Company's Gateway videotex service, all include unmonitored bulletin boards as part of their overall telecommunications service. In many cases, these open boards are potentially the most profitable segments of their information facilities. If they are to be liable for any information that appears on their computers, however, they might as well shut down the bulletin boards; and in that case, since the databanks themselves are too expensive for most individuals' pocketbooks, the broad public audience they hope for will never materialize.

If you have never dealt with, or accessed, as they say in computerland, any of the CBBs, you are apt to wonder why they are so popular, freebies and enticing illegalities aside.

There is no definitive answer to that riddle. The adolescent telephone habit no doubt has something to do with it. Anonymity in an amorphous society, too, plays a role. Ask any reformed bulletin board junkie, like Dave Winer, who used to spend upwards of $500 a month reaching out to unseen computerists via bulletin boards. "It was addicting to communicate with people without any physical contact," he recalls. "I got off the habit because I couldn't afford it." Now, as president of Living Videotext, the company that developed the outline processor Think Tank, he can, but is too busy.

Over and over again, you will hear such comments as "It's not threatening. . . . It's a convenient way to meet people. . . . There's a feeling of community. . . . I can live out my fantasies."

Perhaps it's all a passing fad, a technoacceptable way of meeting new people, as CBs were a few years ago. Perhaps it will develop into a whole new communications network. Only time and the law will tell.

As for myself, I find stuttering away at a screen by means of a keyboard a less than inspiring way of conversing. Ideally, I like to be face to face with the people to whom I am talking. I don't even care for plain, ordinary, unlinked-to-the-computer telephones all that much. What I really needed a modem for was to equip my computer to send my weekly columns down to *The New York Times*'s computer. Realizing this goal, however, was apparently going to entail guiding Tanya away from the engrossing electronic Wonderland into which she seemed to be fast vanishing. It was also going to mean delving more deeply into the software.

Normally, we think of software either in terms of specific applications, such as word processing, or in terms of the systems software, such as DOS, that runs and coordinates (much as a conductor directs an orchestra) the disk drives, printers, and other components of our computer systems. But there is yet another category of software, one often overlooked, that is required to operate independent peripherals like modems that have their own built-in microprocessors.

In essence, such software is a superoperating system, functionally linking your modem, for instance, with all the other equipment you have been collecting ever since you first bought the basic computer itself. Without good communications software, you have a "dumb" terminal. In other words, you can read and write but not process information on the computer screen. I could type this book into the computer, and it could be transmitted over the telephone lines to a receiving computer, character by character. However, slow typist that I am, I would not only be tying up the phone for a number of hours, but incurring a staggering telephone bill as well.

Here is where "smart" modem software enters into the picture. Besides controlling the rudimentary transmission of computer information over the telephone lines, it enables a modem, among other things, to route and shape information for a printer and disk drives as well as to pick up incoming information and store it temporarily in the computer itself, until there is time to put it on disk. This ability both to "upload" and to "download" is one of the first features to check for in communications software.

Uploading capability means that if you have a batch of information on disk, identified by the file name, or label, T5-15-4.32, let's say, you can, with one or two keystrokes, instruct the computer to read that particular file on the disk and send all the information in it directly out the computer communications port and through the modem onto the telephone line. You can also type a message, correct any errors you see in it, store it on disk, and then, perhaps at a later time, when the telephone rates are low, have the computer load the message from the disk and send off your electronic mail.

Downloading is the reverse procedure, whereby your computer receives, via the modem, information sent over the telephone line and records it directly on disk. Surprisingly, a number of communications packages are still being offered without the downloading feature, even though downloading is probably the most important part of a communications package for anyone planning to use either commercial data bases or information banks.

When you have a computer equipped to download, instead of either having to read what is on screen line by line as the information comes in over the telephone or having your printer make hard copy the same way, you can merely request the computer to put all incoming information into its buffer, or electronic holding tank. From there the information can be stored on disk for later use.

Thus, in theory, a student writing a paper on, say, the development of technology in the eighteenth century could request information on Ned Ludd from a data bank, have the facts downloaded and stored on disk, and then, when using his word processor to write the actual report, incorporate quotes taken electronically from this disk directly into his own writing. Hopefully, he would add quotation marks and cite his sources. But that's another problem.

Crosstalk XVI, the communications software included in the Novation communications package, is what is known in the trade as a powerful program. In ordinary language, what this means is that it has a lot of features and can do a lot of things.

There are on the market communications packages that are

much simpler to use, but they are also much more limited. One such easy-to-use program, PFS:Access, puts you effortlessly in touch with other computers in order to obtain information. However, the current version does not allow you to send information, which is the flip side of the communications coin, and the one usually more difficult to deal with.

For Novation's Access 1-2-3, several extra features have been added to Crosstalk's already powerful sending and receiving capabilities. Among these is an on-line/off-line status indicator, appearing in the upper right-hand corner of the screen, which shows whether or not your computer is currently connected with another computer. This is such an obviously useful feature that it might come as a suprise to learn how many of today's communications programs leave you in the dark as to the connection status.

Useful, too, are the so-called command files that appear as you prepare to send out information. On the lower third of the main, or status, screen are listed the prerecorded sets of instructions for your computer. On the command line at the very bottom of the screen appear the words, "Enter number of file to use." Choose your number, and with that single keystroke or two the computer is ready to do all the work of reaching the source designated by that number. Enter an 8, for example, and your machine will automatically dial and connect you with the information utility CompuServe. A 6 will put you in touch with Novation's twenty-four-hour free computer service.

Better yet, you can enter your own command files for accessing remote computers that you intend to have your computer contact often. Since I wanted Tanya to transmit a column to the *Times*, she began preparing a new command file for it. To do so, she first had to set the communications parameters of the software to match those of the receiving computer.

This is where most people starting out in telecommunications stumble. There's a long inventory of parameters, such as baud rate, parity, duplex, data bits, stop bits, and so forth that need to be either checked or changed before your computer can begin to deal with a distant one. In short, the two computers must be on the same wavelength, as hip talk used to have it, in order to communicate, and rarely can they do so without a certain amount of adjustment.

Supposedly to facilitate an understanding of how to set these parameters, people are usually treated to a discourse on the variability of the number of bits per second to be transferred, data timing, integrity checks, and a number of other intricate transmission mechanisms. As interesting as all this information may be technically, most people simply do not want it. Understandably enough, what they want is to be able to use their computers, not to comprehend all their intricacies.

I was reflecting on this inherent tendency toward utilitarianism in most people as Tanya was calling Howard Angione, technical editor of the *Times,* to find out how to induce our computer to talk to his. With the status display in front of her, she entered, in the designated places, first the computer's telephone number as given her by Mr. Angione, then the baud rate, the number of data and stop bits, and the other requisite parameter information—just as if she were entering an extra-long telephone number. When you consider the matter, that's not a bad way of conceptualizing what is involved in calling up another computer.

In this age of Sprint, MCI, and similar special telephone numbers, which have taken us far beyond the recent tradition of dialing 1 followed by an area code and seven digits, thinking of all those settings like 300 for baud rate and 7 for data bits as simply parts of a very long telephone number is refreshingly unintimidating. If you don't know exactly why you are setting the data bit parameter to 7, is that so very different from not knowing precisely what happens when you dial a 1 before a number in those telephone systems requiring it?

With all the parameters entered in their proper places, Tanya typed in the transmitting command XMIT and the name of the file to be shipped out over the wires. The screen lit up with boxes labeled Percent Complete, Consecutive Errors, and Total Errors, and the computer began to reach out and touch something. Unfortunately, according to the screen, what it succeeded in transmitting was nothing but errors.

Tanya cut the connection and went back to the status

screen to see if perchance she had entered a wrong number somewhere. Sure enough, there were 8 data bits instead of the 7 there were supposed to be. She corrected the mistake and began transmitting again.

Once more nothing but errors left the computer. Once more Tanya checked the screen. Once more the data bit setting was 8.

The push-me-pull-me tug of war between Tanya and the machine continued for half a dozen rounds. Finally she tossed in the towel and called the Novation help line again.

This time it turned out that she was reading the wrong section of the 300-page manual. Crosstalk uses two different commands for transmitting files. XMIT is the proper directive if the computer is dealing with another computer likewise equipped with Crosstalk; SEND is the command to be used for all the rest of the computer community. Whenever XMIT is used, the software automatically puts the data bit setting to 8, no matter what you want.

Back to the keyboard with the new command went Tanya. Again transmission failed.

Tanya made a series of unkind remarks about the computer's lack of intelligence, accusations which I assured her were true enough, since in fact the machine has none of that particular attribute. Then she dialed the help line once more and found out one more little secret.

The manual specified sending text files. So, because what she was trying to send was an article, which was obviously text, she assumed that the data would present no problems. What the manual presumed she knew, and thus did not specifically state, was that the file had to be in ASCII code, the American Standard Code for Information Interchange. Because the word processing program I use is written in a different code, the modem, if it is to send the results of my literary labors over the telephone, must restructure the material into ASCII.

Demonstrating the keystrokes required to convert the file, I let Tanya loose among the computer commands once more. By now she could get Crosstalk up and running almost with her eyes closed, and certainly faster than I could.

This time everything worked the way it was supposed to

213

work, and after a few minutes the *Times* computer echoed a message to mine, stating where in its immense memory banks it had tucked away my prose and on which printer my editor —the real one, not the one on disk—could call the story up. All that was left for me to do was to call the editor and let him know that my story was on file. Now that was a bit of a come-down. As Tanya pointed out, how come the computer didn't let him know?

"You still need people for something," I replied. Then, watching her instructing the computer, once more free for action, to dial up yet another bulletin board, I added, "At least to pay the telephone bills."

13: PC Future

It was a cold and snowy December night some nine years after the publication of *Popular Electronics*'s cover story on the Altair that had started it all. The various members of my family were scattered on couches and rugs among the purring cats and the dog chasing rabbits in his dream before the blazing fire. I closed the book I had been reading aloud on my thumb just as Mrs. Cratchit entered with the flaming pudding "like a speckled cannon-ball," a pudding with which no one, least of all Tiny Tim, could find fault.

In the ensuing silence, broken only by the sounds of soft breathing and crackling flames, my mind began to wander along the long roads of technology, particularly that broad avenue of consumer consumption mapped out since Dickens's time, on which he would surely have lost his way in wonderment. All around us were refrigerators, stereos, electric lights, central heating, plumbing—part of my childhood having been spent in a dwelling with an outhouse, a warm bathroom has its own very special technological appeal for me on a dark and crunching-snow-filled winter's eve.

My reflections shifted to the study lying a scant four hundred feet from the house, farther by quite a bit than the usual outhouse. To think that with some dozen odd micro-computers sitting helter-skelter on various desks, chairs, and crates over there, waiting to be unpacked and reviewed, I probably had more computing power at my disposal than that available to the combined military forces of both sides in the Korean conflict. Yet I was still puzzling over what to really and truly do with all that power.

Personal computers for the home, bearing the implied chastisement *Plug In or Drop Out,* may well prove to have been the pinnacle in consumer goods marketing for this decade. Note that I specify computers for the home. Personal computers for business and scientific research are a different matter entirely, although there is more than a little psychosocial fraud involved in the promotion of these as well. But home is where the computer hype really lies.

Checkbook balancing and family financial management are certainly things that a personal computer can do. The computer's processing, furthermore, has an air of accuracy and importance about it. But surely these accomplishments are overly vaunted. Whose computer, after all, is ever going to be assigned such tasks? Most people, myself included, do a rather haphazard job of balancing their checkbooks as it is. To expect them to hunker down and transfer all that hastily scribbled data from check register to computer on a regular basis is something of which only an ardent software enthusiast could conceive.

Carry the zeal a few steps further, and you will meet its epitome in Roy Mason, owner of a futuristic electronic home, Xanadu, in Orlando, Florida. His superinsulated, molded polyurethane abode embodies all kinds of energy-saving concepts, but at its heart lies the electronic hearth. Here is, allegedly, a way to return to the golden days of yore while at the same time moving forward into the exciting world of super-tech. The electronic hearth is "a home computer that is the center of the family's activities—entertainment, bookkeeping, meal planning."

Entertainment, yes, I'll agree with that, but why are those other, serious tasks like constructing a proper diet always creeping into the computer picture? Are they attempts to legitimize the place of the computer in the home, to supplant the frivolity of games? Probably. Yet they simply are not convincing.

Home computers persist in being no more than glorified game machines, and they are likely to remain such, except, of course, for those already beginning to gather dust in the closet along with the CB, the radio scanner, the food processor, and the electric carving knife—remember that one? The reason for their early retirement is a simple one. Computers are designed for information processing, and information is something of which we all have a great surfeit. It may not necessarily be the right information or the information we want. The computer is not going to solve that dilemma for us. It can only process it. Now is a processed predicament really an improvement over an unprocessed one?

But what about education? What about computer literacy? Don't we all need to understand computers? This question I would answer with another: Do we all understand how cars and stereos and telephones and even toasters work? Do we need to, in order to use them?

Of course not. Yet seemingly we must know a lot about personal computers in order to operate them. That is precisely the problem—and it's the computers' problem, not ours. The computer industry tries to shift all the problems it encounters away from the machines and onto the broader shoulders of humanity. That's so much easier than trying to provide solutions for the machines themselves. Its strategy does not, however, alter the actuality that personal computers as they now stand are klutzy, crude devices being foisted off as marvelous must-haves for all those who care about their own and their children's future.

One reason for the emphasis on children in the promotional campaign of the personal computer—how readily they take to computers is repeatedly pointed out—can be found in the fact that children, not yet fully formed in their intellectual capacities, are much more easily bent to the machine's will than are adults. The computer priesthood is today's new Jesuit society. Give them a child early enough, and that child is theirs for life. For what sets the technology of computers apart from that of all man's previous endeavors in individual extension and material control, efforts designed to envelop him in comfort and even pleasure, is that computers instead bend man to their form.

Look at language. Computer science sees it as a means of communication, which it is, of course. But human language is intuitive, poetic in its nature, culturally rich in connotative as well as denotative meaning. Learning and feeling these nuances and shades of meaning are the domain of basic literacy. Yet such richness is wholly at odds with the logic required by computers. Instead of thought-provoking ambiguities, binary absolutes guide the computer-led student.

The world of computers is one of true/false decisions, a universe in which gradations and multiple alternatives, calling for selective interpretation and moral choice, are altogether absent. In the mind of the machine, all things which have existence are computable. By definition, myth is excluded. But the real world is not like that. Thus it is that computer literacy fails the young resoundingly.

On a higher educational plateau, there are some very useful applications for personal computers. However, these lie at the further reaches of the instructional process, in scientific, technical, and engineering courses at the high school or college level.

The present attempt to utilize computers in the education of younger children, at home or at school, is reminiscent in many ways of the teaching machines of the late fifties and early sixties. Forgotten history now, except in the memories of investors who made and lost fortunes on the stock of U.S. Industries, manufacturer of these mechanical substitute teachers, they failed because they did not teach. Neither do computers today.

Learning to move a turtle on the screen is learning a game. Shooting down an invading spaceship labeled 2 × 12 by entering 24 is a game. It seems as if the vast majority of the

218

educational software is being designed by the originators of video games.

Not only that, but some schools are even moving pure put-your-quarter-in arcade games right into their classrooms. San Jose High in California, for instance, settled Centipede, Donkey Kong, and friends comfortably into the school so the kids wouldn't have to walk over to the nearby commercial arcades during class breaks. As the principal explained, "This way they're making an investment in the school."

The assistant principal had an even better argument. "How much time did you spend sitting in the library during breaks? You socialized. You sat down and talked to your friends." Now, instead of socializing with classmates, you can socialize with a computer.

I have nothing against computer games per se. But they are not an education, either literally, in the academic sense, or in the humanistic sense of successfully integrating the individual into the larger society as a whole.

Apart from games, moreover, I can see no function in the home that can truly be served well by personal computers. Of course, the essentially frolicsome nature of the personal computer as would-be homebody could be changed. The checkbook register, to return to one of the industry's most overused examples, could be made part of the computer with the proper software and a bit of hardware finesse. As one wrote out checks, all the vital information could be recorded on a battery-powered credit-card-sized memory unit. Then, once a month, one could simply thrust the whole checkbook into the computer, and it would do all the bookkeeping, tax records preparation, and even monitoring of a budget, if you really wanted it to, automatically.

Such effortless applications are not yet in evidence, however. The telephone made communication easier and more convenient. There were no more embarrassing spelling or grammatical errors to worry about, no more indecipherable handwriting, no more searching for a stamp or fighting one's way through the cold, or the heat, to find a mailbox. One could simply pick up the telephone. The response was instant, to boot.

Word processing for the home tries to do the same thing.

219

Your personal computer can now correct spelling, if not yet grammatical errors, which in fact its software documentation tends to compound. Its printing is reasonably clear. A modem can even send your perfectly composed messages right over the telephone lines.

As if it had sensed my thoughts, the telephone interrupted my fireside reflections abruptly with its shrill peal. The call was from an old friend planning to drop by in a few weeks. We chatted awhile, in the unstructured, rambling, comfortable fashion that the telephone has come to foster—about what we had been doing, and who was where, and how the winter was finally catching up with us.

As I hung up, what came to mind was how much more mail I receive these days, yet how many fewer letters, real letters, make their way into our mailbox. Even international friends are almost as likely to use the telephone as to write.

What future is there for electronic mail in a world already at home with the instant, "user friendly" communication of two-way telephony? Personal word processing, indeed. "Bah! Humbug!" I muttered to the assembled sleeping muses as I sat down in my chair by the fire once more.

I fail to see how home computers, except for hobbyists and workaholics hustling their briefcase portables from the office to the den, can fail to go the way of the Stanley Steamer. But in the same way that automobiles have become a dominant force in our culture—sans steam—computers will become all-pervasive in the home. We just won't know they are there.

Already, dedicated computers, those designed to perform a single set of tasks, are to be found throughout the home. Smart washing machines, smart microwave ovens, smart burglar alarms, smart video cassette recorders—you name the appliance, and the latest model probably has a built-in microcomputer. It's simply not the all-purpose variety the personal computer manufacturers are selling and the early pundits saw as being Everyman's universal tool.

Where the home computer per se may still be in evidence, however, is on the entertainment front. The bloom is off the video game rose, but a new spring will burst forth in a few short years, when the home computer will be wedded to video recording technology in order to take advantage of that medium's incredible imformation storage capacity.

This marriage of computer and video came to me recently in a flight of fancy. Then I was startled to learn that the concept had gone well beyond fantasy among researchers. Some of them have already developed working systems, albeit crude ones. Surprisingly, they use video disks rather than video cassette recorders, or VCRs, for storing their images.

VCRs have more or less trampled video disk systems to death in the marketplace, for one simple reason. You can copy programs off your television screen onto blank cassette tapes. You cannot do this with video disks.

On the other hand, the very fact that replicas of a video disk cannot readily be made contributes a great deal to the disk's potential popularity among software firms, plagued by pirates. Illegal copies are an increasing menace to program producers' profits. The selling of software on video disks would eliminate this problem, at least temporarily.

Another advantage video disks have over video tapes for software is fast memory retrieval. Called upon to find information at the beginning, then near the end, then again toward the beginning of a series of data, a computer using tape must wait while the ribbon is spooled back and forth, a very time-consuming process. Using a video disk for data storage, a computer can pick out information very quickly, from any part of the disk, in any sequence.

The amount of information a single video disk can hold is truly staggering. It can store two gigabytes of data on a side, for a total of four gigabytes, or four billion characters. That is equivalent to the storage capacity of roughly 5,000 double-density floppy disks. Stated in a different way, it is the equivalent of 500,000 pages of typed text.

But because video disks were originally designed to hold images, the real breakthrough in the merger of the personal computer and the video disk lies in the visual realm. A demonstration of the image-handling terminal resulting from their conjunction can be seen at Disney's Epcot Center in Florida. The display uses a touch screen to carry the user along. Touch one of the selections listed on the video screen, and

221

the appropriate images are called up in any sequence you desire. At Epcot, you can even create your own roller coaster on screen. You yourself control the course of the visual ride.

A more complex coupling of video images and action in the real world has been developed by Dr. Myron Krueger of the University of Connecticut and is chronicled in his book, *Artificial Reality*. With the aid of several high-speed computers, he has created a playful graphic creature that darts around your image on the video screen, at times hiding behind your back, reacting to all your movements as picked up by the computer system via video camera.

Take Dr. Krueger's process but a few steps further and you have the personal computer game room of the future. You stand surrounded by four small video cameras hooked up to feed their received images to your computer. A video recorder with a disk of Star Raiders, Murder in the Mansion, or whatever other game you select is also connected to the computer. As the game, say Murder in the Mansion, begins, the image of an old Victorian house on a hill appears on the video projection screen occupying the entire wall opposite you. A camera switches on as you start walking in place. Suddenly you appear walking on the road leading to the mansion.

The computer has taken the camera's image of you, masked out the background, overlaid it onto the frames of the disk, and synchronized the two representations so that they are one.

You notice a wallet on the ground. Stooping, you grasp at the floor. Your video doppelganger reaches into the grass. As you see yourself touch the wallet, you pick it up. A shot rings out in the mansion. You hurry on up the road, no longer playing a game, but living it.

The future is exciting in many ways, but why are we in such a rush to meet it? Pandora's box, having been opened, spews forth a never-ending stream of technology. The question no one seems to be asking is, where will all this technology take us? In a world unprecedentedly polluted with PCBs, mercury, pesticides, and radioactive material in search of a place to be buried safely for 50,000 years, is the course of electronics perhaps leading up to a new pollution, one of the mind, one in which the very imagination that engendered it becomes its victim?

I opened Dickens's *A Christmas Carol* once more and gazed at the book's copperplate frontispiece, alive with the motion of the light and shadow cast by the flickering flames from the fire. As I did so, the imagined voice of a boy whom I have always envisioned as a modern-day Tiny Tim came to mind. He was being interviewed by a BBC survey team on his preferences in entertainment. Though I only heard of the event thirdhand, the picture in my mind has an alternately stern and cajoling Fagin-like character conducting the interview. "Which do you prefer," he asks, "television or radio?"

"Radio, sir."

"Radio? Why is that?"

"The pictures, sir. The pictures are oh, ever so much better."

• • •

There is one place where the picture has definitely been made better by personal computers, and that is in the world of business. Personal computing has irrefutably and irrevocably changed American business, even down to the small cottage and garage enterprise. Its influence will no doubt remain with us well into the foreseeable future—until the power grids collapse and we are all returned to digitizing on our fingers. But even among the executive desks and general-store cash registers, I look at the future through a monitor darkly.

Business software will soon include English language parsers, programs that analyze and interpret statements entered in ordinary language and translate them for the computer. One's being able to enter one's commands to the machine in English instead of an artificial command language will make the computer far easier to use. And quantity of use is, for most people, directly proportionate to ease of use.

The fact that something is easier, however, does not necessarily mean that it is better. Where the computer is concerned, fascination reigns, for man is still in awe of his creation. Slowly, like Narcissus, we are becoming trapped by

223

our own reflection in the monitor. Computer-generated answers, and even questions, are seldom challenged. Somehow the machines we have created seem better, more reliable, than we ourselves.

But they aren't, of course. People program computers. People enter new data into computers. People design models. People make errors, and the machine amplifies them.

People have dreams too, and perhaps one day computers will amplify those as well. Meanwhile, people have fun sometimes, which is as it should be. Not all of life should be tasks, nor all our baggage tools. And if personal computers seem to bring out an ambivalence in me, perhaps it is because, like others facing a future they feel has come too soon, my heart belongs to the eighteenth century, my spirit to the nineteenth, and only my mind to the twentieth. Nevertheless, when all is said and done, I must admit I find the personal computer to be, at the very least, fascinating. After all, a toaster is only a toaster, but a personal computer is a toy.